VERDE RIVER

RECREATION GUIDE

by

Jim Slingluff

GOLDEN WEST ☼ **PUBLISHERS**

Covers designed by Bruce Robert Fischer / The Book Studio
Front cover: Jim Slingluff paddling at Prefalls on the Verde River. (Photo by Wayne House)
Photos not otherwise credited were taken by the author.

CAVEAT

(Warning)

Portions of the Verde River under discussion in this book lie in areas which may be under jurisdiction of the State of Arizona, the federal government, various Indian tribal authorities, or private ownership. Laws and regulations for each of these jurisdictions differ. Land ownership must be respected by persons who use the Verde River for recreational purposes.

Physical hazards may be encountered in areas of the Verde River and its tributaries. Water conditions change from day to day. Readers should take cognizance of the safety precautions identified in this book, as author and publishers cannot accept responsibility for such matters.

This book cannot replace lessons under a competent paddler. It cannot replace studying a quality instruction video or reading a book written to teach canoeing. It *can* give you some advice on how to avoid bad times on the water, but you will need to determine whether or not you find yourself in a bad situation.

Library of Congress Cataloging-in-Publication Data
Slingluff, Jim
    Verde River recreation guide / Jim Slingluff.
    Includes bibliographical references (p.) and index.
    1. Canoes and canoeing—Arizona—Verde River—Guide-books.
    2. Kayaking—Arizona—Verde River—Guide-books. 3. Outdoor recreation—Arizona—Verde River Region—Guide-books.
    4. Verde River Region (Ariz.)—Description and travel—Guide-books. I. Title
GV776.A62V477 1990   797.1'22'0979157—dc20   90-45887
ISBN 0-915846-50-7   CIP

Printed in the United States of America

2nd Printing ©1993

GOLDEN WEST PUBLISHERS
4113 N. Longview Ave. • Phoenix, AZ 85014, USA • (602) 265-4392

Dedication

To the people of the Verde Valley. You hold more potential influence over the future of the Verde than anyone else.

To the employees of Arizona Game and Fish Department, Arizona State Parks, and the U.S. Forest Service who labor to protect the Verde for its ecological and recreational values.

To John Parsons, who has given more than any other single person to the cause of creating a constituency for the Verde River.

SAFETY TIPS

- Unless you are a very competent intermediate boater—capable of running Class 3 water—do not paddle a wilderness section alone or as trip leader. Your best bet is to run it first with someone who has run it at the level and in the conditions you expect to encounter. If you do go into a section that you do not know well, remember that the minimum number of boats for a "safe" trip is three.
- Watch the weather.
- Do not drink or take mind-altering substances while paddling.
- Don't expose yourself or your loved ones to pointless risk.
- Read and follow the recommendations in the chapter "Being Safe and Happy on the River."

Foreword

The Verde River and its major tributaries such as Oak Creek, Wet Beaver Creek and West Clear Creek are some of Arizona's most valuable natural resources. One of the Southwest's longest stretches of free-flowing river, the Verde River supports an amazing variety of threatened species.

Surprisingly, it is also accessible to a large percentage of Arizona's population, which makes it one of our most notable recreation resources, too. Whether your preference is a tranquil picnic on the banks of the Verde at Deadhorse Ranch State Park in Cottonwood, or Class 3 whitewater in the Wild & Scenic portion of the river above Horseshoe Lake, the Verde provides a wide range of outdoor experiences suitable for the day tripper or the serious backcountry traveler.

This book is an excellent introduction to the Verde River and the wide variety of natural and cultural experiences it has to offer. It takes the reader on a descent down the Verde River from its headwaters to its confluence with the Salt River, taking the time to explore some of the major side tributaries while it touches on various items of local interest, such as topical environmental issues, natural history and cultural anthropology.

It is intended to serve as an introductory guide to the area, whether you are a casual traveler or serious backcountry enthusiast. The sections on camping, boating, river resources, outfitters and outdoor organizations will be useful to all who wish to learn or do more with the Verde. The book is well-organized, easy to read and provides an excellent introduction to river ecology.

It is obvious that the author is entranced by the Verde River and all it has to offer. His love and appreciation for the special resources of the Verde River system brings to the reader a sense of intimacy and familiarity that one rarely finds in a guide of this sort. Jim knows the Verde River and we are fortunate that he has found the time to share his knowledge with us. With luck, we'll see more of the same for Arizona's other special rivers and streams.

Andy Laurenzi
President, Arizona Riparian Council

Introduction

This is a celebration of and a guide to the Verde River and its major tributaries. It is written to be helpful to a wide variety of recreationists.

I hike, hunt, fish, paddle canoes, watch birds and wildlife, and pay some attention to geology and plants. I've tried to weave threads from all these areas into this book without making the book a text on any one of them. Recreationists vary not only in what they like to do but in the intensity with which they like to do it. I've geared this book to recreationists of casual and intermediate skills.

There is the strong flavor of human-powered boats to this. Human-powered boats, especially plastic canoes, permit one to visit the Verde with very light impact. Canoes, and other human-powered boats, create no new trails nor do they contribute to the erosion of existing ones. What disturbance of the stream bottom that does occur is erased by the next cycle of high water. Boaters enjoy certain legal advantages, as well as being able to take a little bit extra in gear.

The book is more than a boating guide. I also discuss the creek with an eye toward the informational needs of hikers, horsemen and car campers.

Verde River Recreation Guide differs from most guide books in that it is not just a factual description of the Verde and its tributaries. I tell stories, also. Stories which are designed to give you an intuitive feel for the watershed, even if you never actually travel any of these waterways.

Like most boaters, I like my streams made interesting with rocks, current, and various obstructions. I have spiced the book with "eddies" of various sizes. These "eddies" discuss topics of special interest concerning the Verde and its environs.

I have personally paddled a canoe down the entire perennial portion of the Verde and significant sections of its major tributaries. I've canoed the Verde and its tributaries in all seasons and at a wide variety of water flow. I have also hiked many of the tributaries.

I have had a great deal of pleasure discovering some of the special secrets of the Verde watershed and I'm going to present you with that same opportunity.

The Verde watershed offers incredible variety and beauty. We are fortunate to have it. Enjoy it! Take care of it!

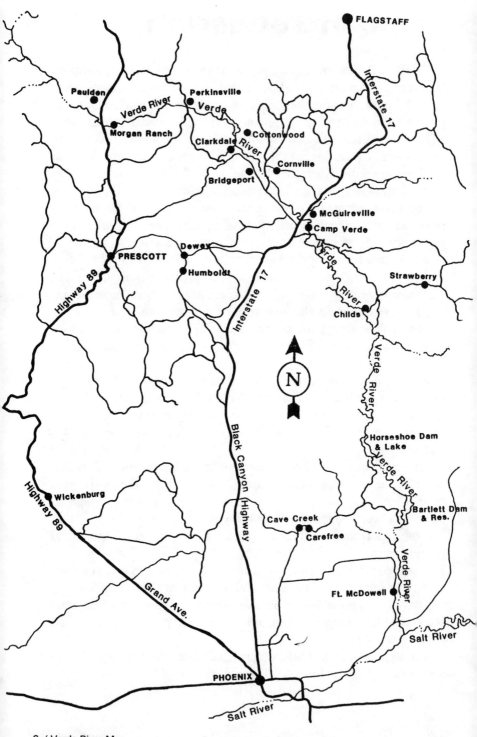

Contents

Maps

Being Safe and Happy on the River

This book cannot replace lessons under a competent paddler. It can't replace studying a quality instructional video or reading a book written to teach canoeing. It can give you some advice on how to avoid bad times on the water. **You, though, will determine whether or not you find yourself in a "bad situation."**

Before you put on the river. . .

Know something about the section you intend to paddle and the conditions you can expect to encounter. Read this book. Talk to the Forest Rangers. Talk to other paddlers. Look at some topographical (topo) maps. Call the Salt River Project to find the flow levels. Check out weather reports. After you know something about what you face, you can plan your trip and choose your paddling companions more intelligently.

Most of the people I've met on the river who were not having a good time were victims of their own bad planning. Some of them had no idea how many miles they had obligated themselves to travel. Others held wildly inaccurate beliefs on how far they could travel in one day.

Still others somehow forgot that it takes time to drive to the river and load the boats. The saddest of all were those who committed one or more of the above mistakes and decided to bring along people even more inexperienced than themselves.

Unless you are a very competent intermediate boater—capable of running Class 3 water—do not paddle a wilderness section alone or as trip leader. Your best bet is to run it first with someone who has run it at the level and in the conditions you expect to encounter. If you do go into a section that you do not know well, remember that the minimum number of boats for a "safe" trip is three.

Learn to read topo maps and understand what that information says about the river. The greater the drop in elevation per mile, the more likely you are to encounter swift current and rapids, especially at high flows.

Tributaries, including washes that fall quickly to the river and which also drain a good-sized watershed, will usually create a rapid immediately below their juncture with the Verde. Topos are unreliable regarding islands. Many of the islands shown on the topo maps exist only at very high water, if at all. Some islands that do exist are not shown. The river changes its terrain constantly.

Unless you know otherwise, from experience, plan to cover no more than 10 miles per full day on the river. Why hurry?

Like Santa Claus, be making your lists and checking them twice. Make sure the items on your list make it into the boats.

> **Watch the weather.** Especially watch for conditions that may raise the water level. The three situations you will want to watch most closely are summer monsoons, hard and lengthy rains, hard and lengthy rains on a snow pack in the high country.

Once on the river...

Watch and listen to what is going on. Rapids are usually announced by changes in landscape and in sound. It is not really the loudness of the rapid that is telling. It is the depth of the sound. Riffles can be loud, but not deep. Deep and loud is a sure sign that you should pay close attention.

Visually, watch for any change in the size or distribution of the stream bank boulders. Watch the banks for evidence that a tributary or wash is about to enter. All rivers are liquid energy moving downhill. A pool is simply stored energy, energy that must eventually be released in a downhill run or rapid. The larger the pool, the greater the stored energy. The greater the stored energy, the greater chance of a significant rapid.

Do not drink or take mind-altering substances while paddling. The response time of emergency medical personnel to most of the Verde is generally slow because of the remote conditions.

In cold conditions, alcohol increases the speed with which your body loses heat, thus speeding up the onset of hypothermia. It does this by countering your body's defensive reaction to a drop in your inner body temperature. Your body tries to protect your inner core by decreasing blood flow to your arms and legs. This is why your hands and feet get cold. Alcohol makes you feel warm by increasing blood flow to the extremities, making them feel warm at the expense of the warmth of your heart and lungs.

Coffee or tea work with your body by helping constrict your blood vessels. While this helps maintain your core temperature, it actually makes your hands and feet feel colder than if you had not had any caffeine. Nicotine has the same effect. Your best bet is to drink or eat something hot that also has food value. Your body needs fuel, not stimulation. Some additional hints include:

- Save any arrogance for the card table, especially if you are responsible for other, less skilled people on the trip.
- Never enter a rapid unless you can see the entire way to the end.
- Be very careful near all strainers. They are involved in a large percentage of the very few paddling deaths that occur every year.
- Be particularly careful at the Falls and Prefalls of the Verde. I know of one person who swam the Falls at low levels. He required a dozen stitches.
- When trying to decide whether or not to run a rapid, be influenced by the following:
  1. If you don't run it successfully, you will be required to swim it from whatever point your failure occurs.
  2. In light of point one, no one should run a rapid with which they are uncomfortable.
  3. It is always faster to walk a rapid and line the boat through than it is to clean up after an upset or to attempt to deal with a pin.
  4. Do you want to run the risk of being submerged in water of that temperature and then exposed to air of that temperature? Remember, if air temperature plus water temperature is less than 100 degrees totaled, you face a situation where hypothermia is a present hazard.
- Keep all ropes and lines, especially those with fish hooks attached, well secured.
- If you swamp your boat, stay upstream of it.
- If you are going to face substantial whitewater, put additional flotation in your canoe. Tying inner tubes into the thwarts does nicely.
- Always put your children into quality life jackets. Put yourself into one, also.
- If you find yourself swimming in a rapid, get on your back, get your butt and feet high, and keep your fingers in a fist. You are trying to

minimize the portions of your fragile body that could strike or get stuck between rocks.

- If you are pushed into an obstruction, the water will attempt to seize your upstream edge as soon as your speed is slower than that of the current and flip you over. You can counter this by leaning in such a way as to show the bottom of your craft to the current.
- Do not paddle into a drop that has a vertical drop where the water at the bottom flows back up to the drop (up river). Such drops are called drowning machines, or reversals. They are commonly found below dams where the water flows over the top of dams. The only place they occur with any regularity on the Verde is at the Falls and Prefalls.
- Take along water purification equipment and use it. A wide variety of animals walk, swim, urinate, defecate, die and rot in these waters.
- Boaters slang for a helmet is "brain bucket." I like the term. It clearly states the reason why helmets should be worn. Kayakers and other decked boates should always wear their "brain buckets." Open boaters, canoeists, and inflatable paddlers should wear them whenever they paddle Class 3 or higher water, or whenever dropping over waterfalls.
- Life jackets. Sitting on life jackets, or using them as pillows causes them to lose buoyance. Treating your life jacket this way is similar to cutting strips from your parachute in order to wipe sweat from your brow. I suggest you require all children to wear life jackets.

It will only be through trial and error that you will be able to learn what cubic feet per second (cfs) levels are safe for you and how you must outfit your boat to meet the challenges provided at each level.

Don't expose yourself or your loved ones to pointless risk. Start exploring segments in very shallow conditions and expect to do some wading. Once you know the construction of the stream, you can better estimate the cfs levels that are safe for you. For your information, all photos of canoeists in this book show the river at levels above 50 cfs but below 100 cfs on the Camp Verde gauge.

Overview of the Verde Watershed

Geology and Prehuman Characteristics

Over the eons, the land we call Arizona has been repeatedly inundated by seas. At least four times, the territory now ruled by the Verde River was ocean bottom.

During the Mississippi Era, some 325 or so million years ago, the Redwall Limestone deposits were laid down. These deposits now provide the spectacular beauty of the Perkinsville Canyon, the intimate beauty of the canyon below US Mines, and some of the tallest cliffs of the Grand Canyon.

More recently, during Cenozoic times, what is now the Verde Valley was repeatedly coated by shallow lakes. These were created when the ancient ancestor of the Verde was dammed and dammed again by geological fault movements. Fossils from this era show the area was populated with mastadons, camels, horses, lions, bears and tapirs.

Presently, the Verde is eroding through millions of yesteryear's deposits, uncovering the past more surely than any archeologist or paleontologist.

The Verde flows between the Central Highlands and the Colorado Plateau of Arizona until it cuts through the Central Highlands and joins the Salt River in the Basin and Range country near Phoenix.

Upriver of the Verde Valley, the river flows through and over limestone and basalt. The Verde Valley itself was created by uplifts along the Verde Fault to the south and erosion of the Colorado Plateau to the north. Because of this uplift, some of the rocks on the Black Hills south of the Valley date back to the Precambrian Era. Down river of the valley, Hackberry Mountain once provided volcanic activity, as did the Mazatzals yet further down river.

First Americans

It is thought that the first humans were gathering roots and hunting animals some 12,000 years ago. Out of these people grew the Cochise Culture, which dominated until a couple of hundred years before Christ.

Somewhere around 250 BC, different cultures evolved. The Anasazi culture dominated the northwest plateau. Hohokam colored the deserts, and Mogollon the mountains. Further west, grew a Pai culture and beyond that, near the present day Arizona/California border, the Patayan culture dominated.

Long about 1200 AD, the Anasazi-influenced peoples started moving south. A related culture, the Sinagua, built Tuzigoot, Montezuma Castle, and many other cliff dwellings and pueblos that now stand as ruins along the Verde River.

Some, but not all, of the tribes which now touch the Verde came from those cultures. It is likely that Sinaguas and Anasazis begat the Hopi. The Hohokam begat the Pima and Papago.

The Maricopas are actually related to the tribes along the Colorado River, sharing a Patayan culture background. They started moving in with the Pimas in the 1600s. Over the years, the Pimas and the Maricopas have pretty much merged culturally.

The Yavapais share a Pai cultural background with the Grand Canyon tribes of the Hualapai and Havasupai. The Yavapais are sometimes called the Yavapai-Apache. This is misleading. The Navajo and Apaches are both Athapaskan speakers. Their ancestors migrated from Canada and entered Arizona shortly before the Spanish. The Yavapais had a good bit of interaction with Apache bands and there was substantial cultural borrowing.

Right now the Verde crosses or passes close to three reservations. The Yavapais have a very small reservation near Camp Verde. A mix of Yavapais, Maricopas and Pimas live on the Fort McDowell and Salt River reservations near Phoenix.

Spanish Exploration

The Spanish first touched the Verde in 1583. Antonio de Espejo, while on yet one more search for gold, stopped near the present location of Jerome. In his *Journal*, he describes the river through the Verde Valley as a wide, slow, meandering, marsh-like river. He named it *El Rio do Los Reyes*, The River of the Kings. He was followed in 1598 by Marios Farfgan de Los Godos, who also stopped near the present location of Jerome.

The Spanish legacy for the Verde includes a lost gold mine, called Sierra Azul. In the mid 1700s, Spanish explorers reportedly found a pure, very rich vein of gold at a spot now thought to be some five to ten miles east of Perkinsville. To this day, the area is rugged and remote. Discovered by Apaches, the miners were picked off one by one until they abandoned the mine. Two survivors reached the Spanish settlements to the south, complete with maps. The mine never has been rediscovered.

This part of the world became part of the sovereign country of Mexico when the Mexicans won their independence from Spain. The entire Verde Watershed was taken from Mexico by the United States as part of the settlement of the Mexican War, a war that General U.S. Grant called "The most unjust war every waged by a stronger nation upon a weaker one."

Anglos

In 1826, Anglos arrived. A band of fur trappers were trapping and exploring along the Gila and Salt Rivers. Stumbling over the mouth of the Verde (which was then known as the San Francisco), they sent a party upstream. James Pattie led a group up the Verde to the Chino Valley, and then returned to the main group. Three years later, one of the original group, Ewing Young, returned on another trapping expedition. In his band was a very young Kit Carson. Thirty some years later, Carson was back in Arizona, waging war on the Navajos.

Settlers, attracted to the grass and water, followed trappers to the Verde Valley. (The river was now called the *Verde*, which is Spanish for Green.) Conflicts arose between Native Americans and settlers.

In the mid 1860s, Fort Lincoln was established at the juncture of Beaver Creek and the Verde River. Fort McDowell was established at the same approximate time near the juncture of the Verde and the Salt. In the early 1870s Fort Lincoln was moved a mile or so down stream and named Fort Verde, then Camp Verde. Ruins of this military outpost still exist and can be visited in the town of Camp Verde.

In 1875, about 1500 Yavapais were herded together here and force-marched to a spot near Globe, Arizona. Over 200 died. Many of the survivors returned in the early 1900s. The last Indian battle in the area was fought high on the Mogollon Rim, thirty miles east of Camp Verde in 1881. The site is marked on Forest Maps as Battleground Ridge. Both Camp Verde and Fort McDowell were abandoned in the early 1890s.

As the century turned over, copper mining grew in importance near Jerome. The area was devastated by the effects of acid rain from the smelters. World War I brought boom times and labor difficulties.

Though not as well known as the Bisbee Deportation, a similar deportation of labor union activists took place in Jerome, organized by the mining companies.

It was during this copper boom that the railroad was driven through the Perkinsville canyon and the power plants at Irving, Childs, and Clarkdale were built.

Since the early 1970s there has been an explosive population growth in the Valley. People move here because of the moderate climate and the (fast disappearing) rural lifestyle.

Physical Characteristics of the Verde Watershed

The technical headwaters of the Verde are in the high country near Ash Fork, Arizona, an hour's drive west of Flagstaff. The first perennial flow used to be at Del Rio Springs (Of the River Springs) north of Prescott, in the Chino Valley.

The flow of these springs is now either diverted for irrigation or trapped in the silted remainder of Sullivan Lake. Present day, the highest point of perennial water is a couple of miles below the point where old Rt. 89 crosses Sullivan Lake, near the headquarters of Morgan Ranch.

At first, the Verde flows to the east. This starts to change near the top of the Verde Valley. By the time the river departs the Valley no doubt remains: the river is going south.

For much of its journey, the Verde flows through rugged geography. The Verde never has an urban feel. In fact, it is only rarely you could use the adjective "rural." Overwhelmingly, the Verde and its tributaries penetrate remote and wilderness lands.

The Verde watershed drains 6,646 square miles and collects an average 464,253 acre feet of water per year. Most of this water comes off the Colorado Plateau, the north side of the river. Spectacular canyons are created as tributaries like Sycamore Creek, Oak Creek, Beaver Creek and Fossil Creek try to drain the moist high country.

Different portions of the watershed react with different speed to increases in moisture that need draining. All of the tributaries and the Verde above the Verde Valley will rise a very short time after the runoff starts down the watershed. This wall or wave of water (it can literally be a wall or wave) may not hit the area below Childs for 24 to 48 hours later. Below Horseshoe Dam, water flow is at the whim of the Salt River Project.

The elevation at Morgan Ranch is 4,260. About 195 miles later, at the Salt River, the Verde has cut to 1,320 feet elevation. The Verde is mostly a calm river. The section between Beasley Flats and Childs has the most notable rapids, including Verde Falls. Fallen trees, fences and diversion dams make up the remaining hazards. The river as a whole is Class 2 or lower in difficulty, **except at high flows**.

Much of the Verde is already shallow. Unless present trends are reversed, enough water may be sucked from the watershed to destroy the Verde as a recreation and wildlife resource.

We start our trip up in the Chino Valley, near Morgan Ranch. We will be in a shallow canyon cut into the grasslands and juniper flats common to that altitude. We may very well see antelope on our drive into the river.

See you on the river!

A lone paddler drops down a typical Verde rapid.

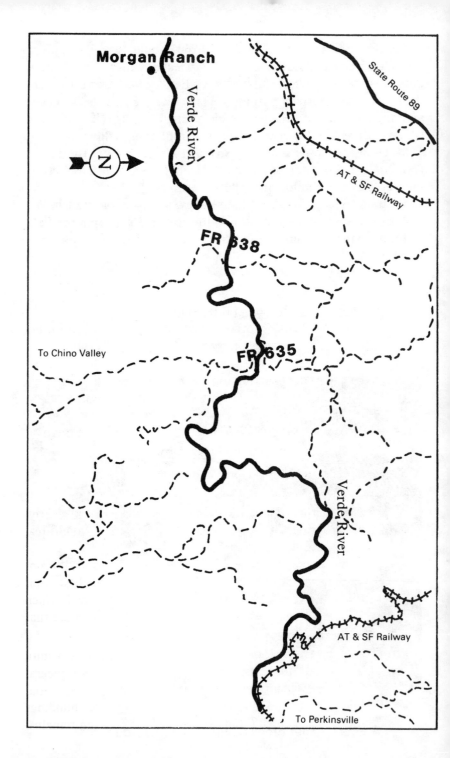

Morgan Ranch to Perkinsville

Mileage: 24 miles

Elevation Change: 4260-3850

Warnings: ● Private land above FR 638.
- Private land at Verde Ranch. FR 635 is closed at property boundaries.
- Scattered fences.
- Some off-road vehicle damage.

Motorized access:
- No public access above FR 638.
- FR 638 is four-wheel drive only from the north. Two-wheel drive access is possible from the south, except when the road is wet.
- US Mines is accessed using a two-wheel drive road (FR 492A) which cuts off from FR 492 on the north side of the river.
- FR 354 or FR 318 into Perkinsville are two-wheel drive unless the road is wet or closed by snow.

Days needed: 2 to 6

We're talking the top of the Verde here. There is a clearly-identifiable river gorge for a few miles above the Morgan Ranch area, but it does not have water in it year 'round.

Even if it did, some of the gorge is so jumbled with rocks, it is not likely that it will ever be boated. Morgan Ranch is the highest point where the Verde flows year 'round and also the highest point at which it can be canoed. There are not many streams that can boast that combination.

From another angle, this section isn't boatable now. Up until Memorial Day, 1989, the ranch owners allowed access to the general public in spite of problems with trash and drunks. That Memorial Day, someone went in and burned down one of their ranch buildings and now the access is gone. I don't blame them. The point remains, you can't get into the Verde above FR 638.

Then why do I discuss it here? It is part of El Rio de Los Reyes. In order to have an accurate picture of the Verde, it's important to know something about the entire perennial section. Habitats don't start and stop at property lines. This isn't solely a guide book. It's an effort to help you understand the flow and world of this beautiful and important riparian area.

At the top of the Verde is a still, mile-long, curving pool.

Below the pool, the creek flows through an unboatable stretch of marsh grass, perhaps 100 yards long. In October, we dragged the boats through, becoming boaters again as we hit the backwaters of the first of the beaver dams.

Starting below the first dam, and extending for well over a mile, both banks were bordered with thick blankets of four-foot high sunflowers. At times the creek was only inches deep and four feet wide while the flower beds were twice that width or more. We were truly paddling the flowers. The wings of the bees gave us our musical score. The butterflies provided the dance.

After a mile or so into the trip, the river cuts down into the land creating small banks. The loss of the marshy bank also meant the loss of the flowers. There is significant thermal impact to the water in this section of river, with the water often remaining above 55 degrees Fahrenheit. This changes the nature of water vegetation and prevents some amphibians and reptiles from hibernating.

Once the banks start to rise, riparian shrubs rule the banks for miles down stream. They give way only periodically to cliffs or steep talus (a slope at the bottom of a cliff).

About four miles into the trip is a section which has been heavily grazed. The banks have been trampled and the creek gets a bit wider and shallower. The shrubs return a few miles above FR 638. At times they nearly create a tunnel through which the water flows. There are some thick populations of fish wherever you find these conditions, though fishing for them through the stream bank growth presents some difficulties.

Falcons live here, too. Once, my presence startled a covey of quail. At that same instant, a falcon streaked over my head in pursuit of the fleeing prey. Predator and prey both disappeared behind a hill, so I can't tell you the end of the story. I can tell you that the majority of times the prey escapes.

The Verde enters public land a few miles above FR 638. I believe most boaters will prefer to put on further down river at US Mines. Hikers, horsemen and anglers may want to explore the river here.

Down creek from here, the river gorge gains altitude and moves closer to the water. Trees start to invade the bank side territory of the shrubs. Muldoon Canyon enters at TRM 7.5. Nine miles into its journey, the Verde flows under some barbed wire fences and passes onto the private land of the Verde Ranch.

This private holding is small in size. Hikers and horsemen will find it well within their capabilities to climb out of the river bed and walk around this private land. Boaters can legally pass through, though I **really recommend you put on below the Verde Ranch**.

Just below the Ranch, the river splits its meager flow around an island. Neither channel has enough water to paddle (normally), so boaters are faced with dragging their boats over a considerable distance.

If there would be enough water to paddle, you would be swept by the fast current into all sorts of trees and shrubs. FR 638 has no advantages over the roads into US Mines. In fact, I suspect horsemen and hikers will find they prefer to enter downstream also.

After the river heals the split caused by the island, the creek flows through a series of pools separated by shallow runs. The water is bordered with short reeds and flows through a floodplain characterized by rock bars and some sand.

On occasion these rock bars are bordered by grassy fields before the rise of the gorges gives the land over to the junipers and other trees of these elevations. These pools contain large populations of Sonoran Mountain, Sonoran Desert, and Razorback Suckers. These native fish are joined by bass and some nice-sized channel cats.

The mile or so down to King Canyon is worth walking into to visit. In the monsoons, you will find wild flowers along this floodplain. I have chased muskrats down the river and, in this section, I saw my first river otter.

I was hiking along the creek down river from Verde Ranch. As I started to cross, there was a sudden underwater distrubance at the edge of the reeds, five yards upstream.

"Huh," I thought. "Guess I startled a carp or sucker." The water was muddy, but I stopped anyway, hoping to see the fish.

There! I saw the fish come to surface right in front of me, not seven yards away.

"I wonder what that brown seaweed is doing stuck to the neck of the fish."

The fish was dead. The seaweed was alive. It was a young otter with dinner. He swam past me to a partially submerged driftwood pile. Climbing onto the dried and twisted wood, he gave me a brief glance, dove back in the water and swam away.

There used to be a four-wheel drive access at King Canyon from the south side of the river by using a spur off FR 635. This spur traveled down Bull Basin drainage before hitting the river at King Canyon.

There was an unfortunate aspect to this. This beautiful spot of green grass and trees was often befouled by the Driving Destroyers. (Orcs of the contemporary world). Abandoned sleeping bags, used diapers, toilet paper, and beer cans adorned the landscape. Scars inflicted by the bastards mar the hillsides and the riparian zone itself. I have seen careless gunplay here by fools who equate firearms with firecrackers, using them to create noise and light in the dark evening.

There are a few sections in here that have been devastated by the Driving Destroyers. I found an area downstream where every stick of burnable wood had been consigned to the fire. Rather than bring their own firewood in, they had hooked chains up to one lone dead tree and tried to pull it down with their vehicles. The snag won this battle. The chain was wedged so tightly into the tree that it had to be left when the Destroyers went home.

King Canyon is at TRM 11. Below here, the canyon walls really do start to rise, reaching towards 300 feet. A short three miles later you pass Duff Spring on the right and enter a deep narrow canyon that will hold you the four miles to Hell Point.

Nice stuff in here, folks. There is typically a flood plain on at least one side of the river the whole way to Hell Point, so hikers and horsemen can get through here with some wading, but without too much trouble. Boaters will encounter some shallow spots, especially near the powerline crossings, but my memories of this place are mostly of wonder. The cliffs are eroding limestone, and some cliff dwellings nestled up under some of the overhangs. Periodically, the creek flows into quiet, intimate little spots, overhung with trees. There is an impressive amount of beaver sign in here, also, though not many dams.

At Hell Point the Verde picks up a considerable amount of drainage. It is joined by Hell Canyon, and the combined forces of MC Canyon and Bear Canyon. There is private land here, set off by fences. At the time of this writing, the land is not closed. The gates are posted with Forest Service signs asking you to close them. Be courteous and we can keep land access through this parcel.

The debris brought down by all these drainages creates a section of more than a mile where the creek is very shallow. The same interaction of flood water and debris has created some very deep pools, back waters, and secluded spots of peaceful beauty.

Two miles below Hell Point, 19.5 miles into the Verde's descent, is an area known as Bear Siding or US Mines. It is reached by using FR 492A, which turns off FR 492 on the north side of the river. At this point, the Verde enters one of its loveliest sections. Limestone walls of red and white color rise 40 to 100 feet high. The creek, when not bordered by cliffs, sports growths of hackberry, walnut, mesquite and other riparian trees. This section is a favorite of mine because of its intimacy and color.

There are bass, cats and native fish in these waters. Muskrats, beavers and probably otters, swim here, too. I've paddled past javelina within easy handgun range. **Boaters will find that shallow water forces them out of their boats periodically**, but it is a minor price to pay to enjoy this beautiful world.

This canyon ends at TRM 21, where the railroad first becomes visible high on the river left bank. The creek continues to create beauty. As you near the Perkinsville crossing, you pass a number of drainages which are all worth a hike, such as Government Canyon at TRM 22.75, Wildcat Canyon at 23.25, and Munds Draw at 23.75.

The largest beaver dam on the Verde is located at the point where the ditch that waters the Perkinsville Ranch starts. It is, to my knowledge, also the last dam on the Verde. Downstream of here, the river is often tightly gripped by canyons and it picks up considerable drainage. The floods that regularly result from this combination would simply wipe out all the dams. The beavers adjust by building their dams in the banks. They do exist on the Verde main stem below here. Beavers just don't build dams on the main stem. They do build dens on some of the tributaries of the Verde in the Verde Valley.

Down over a couple of drops, paddle through a couple of pools and the bridge at Perkinsville is visible, providing access for boaters and other recreationists.

You and the Verde have now come 24 miles since you began to flow.

Isolated Ranches

All along the remote sections of the Verde, indeed along most western rivers, sit a number of isolated ranches. Reaching these homes, and businesses, by land often means driving many miles over questionable roads. Because of people's tendency to try to live near water, however, recreationists traveling the streams often move quite close to these private homes. Here are some things to remember.

- If these ranchers really wanted people to stop by to visit, or if they wanted a lot of folk gawking at their homes, they would sell out and move into town. Your presence may be tolerated. Don't construe that to be an invitation.
- The response time of 911 out to these ranches is not very good, so many of these ranchers are committed supporters of the Second Amendment. They are often familiar with firearms and have them at ready access. If you go wandering around buildings where you have not been invited, you may remind them of other uninvited visitors who proved to have bad intentions.
- Every rancher has stories of cattle poached, equipment vandalized, and water gaps cut. Much of the problem rests with the outlaw operators of ORV's. Gates will be dismantled so they can get access to drive in and destroy. Trash will be left in heaping mounds.
- Personally, I've never had a bad experience with a landowner or tenant. I have found them all to be courteous individuals, surprisingly resilient after years of bad experiences with uninvited recreationists.

Water Gaps and Grazing Patterns

As you travel down the river, you will periodically encounter fences across the river. These are often barbed wire fences, but are, on occasion, electric or dangling wood. **DO NOT CUT OR DAMAGE THESE FENCES**. Damaging these fences is not a "monkey wrench" blow for the environment. In addition to being a crime, it is a blow **against** the environment.

These sections of fence are called "water gaps." They are of more fragile construction than the fences on land. This allows the periodic floods to wash them out and not create a dam. The rancher must replace them after every flood. The purpose of stringing a water gap across the stream is to keep stock from moving into graze areas that they are not supposed to graze.

If you remove this barrier, you are helping to expose the entire riaprian zone to uncontrolled grazing. Help keep riparian areas in good health, in addition to not worsening landowner relations.

It is not difficult for a boater to get past these fences. They are not driven into the ground, so the boater need only lift and twist the fence a bit to provide enough space through which to float their craft.

If the fence is posted "No Trespassing," hikers and horsemen have no legal option but to turn back or follow the fence line until they can travel around the private property. If the land is not posted, you can legally assume it is OK to proceed unless you are asked to leave. **If you are asked to leave, you must do so.**

Canoe trip starts with camp set-up.

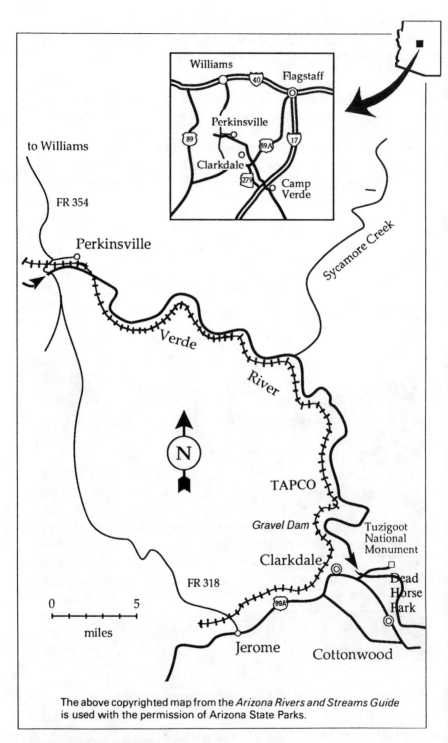

The above copyrighted map from the *Arizona Rivers and Streams Guide* is used with the permission of Arizona State Parks.

Perkinsville to TAPCO

Mileage: 21 miles

Elevation Change: 3850 to 3400

Warnings:
- Private land at Perkinsville, Packard Ranch, and TAPCO (The Arizona Power Company).
- Electric fences across the river in Packard Ranch area.
- Rock pile from landslide blocking all boating passages at the railroad tunnel.
- Rapid at Railroad Draw is dangerous at higher flows. Even at low flows the footing can be tricky.
- Eagle Closures.

Motorized access:
- Perkinsville, using FR 354 or 318.
- TAPCO, using FR 131 off of Tuzigoot Monument Road.
- Access at Sycamore Canyon, controlled by Arizona Game and Fish Department (AGFD). Contact AGFD for details.
- Railroad trips are available through the canyon.

Days needed: Two to however many you can spare.

Perkinsville can be reached using FR 354 out of Williams or FR 318 out of Jerome. These roads meet at Perkinsville (actually, at the Perkinsville river crossing—the Perkinsville train station is a bit farther to the east), so it is possible to drive from Jerome to Williams.

These roads are passable to a two-wheel drive sedan except when wet. If wet enough, these roads will eat a full-sized four-wheel drive up to the chassis. Passable does not mean smooth. It means you need not lose your oil pan, not that you won't.

FR 318 is one of the prettiest dirt roads in Arizona, especially driving from Jerome toward Williams. The road rises to 4,900 feet elevation and offers great views of the Verde Valley, the river gorge, and the mountains outside of Flagstaff and Williams.

On your way into Perkinsville from this direction the road skirts around the upper end of Horseshoe Canyon, which becomes a significant signpost at river level. I've seen lots of wildlife along this forest road, including some huge mule deer.

Perkinsville Crossing is a popular spot with folk from Williams for fishing and camping. **This is private land, so be neat and courteous.** You don't have any right to be here. You have access by courtesy of the landowner. You movie buffs out there might be interested to know that portions of "How the West Was Won" were filmed in this area. Boaters will paddle a narrow, braiding little creek and will be forced out of boat on a few occasions due to downed trees, barbed wire and shallow water. Not far below the crossing is a series of cottonwood trees which sport an extensive heron rookery. I have seen upwards of 20 herons at a time in and near these trees. It's a real kick to watch these long-legged fishermen land on the upper edges of these large trees.

Something like a mile below the river crossing the railroad is trestled from river left to river right. This is where Orchard Draw sometimes dumps large amounts of water and debris into the Verde. It is also the spot where you re-enter public land. The railroad track stays within 60 vertical feet of the river for over ten miles. However, the track is mostly built up on the talus slopes. It is not visually intrusive. From the river level, it is barely noticeable.

Below the trestle, limestone cliffs advance toward the river as the flood plain begins to disappear. They move in close, then recede a bit as Horseshoe Canyon approaches a little over two miles below the trestle. In this two plus miles the creek alternates between being shallow and rocky, and then having deep pools. The cliffs visually rise about 400 feet above the creek. Out of eyesight, the land continues its rise through the juniper flats, the ponderosa forests, the aspens, and the firs until it reaches the high, dry tundra of the San Francisco Peaks.

This section is wonderful. Beautiful water filled with native suckers, chubs and spikedace minnows. Bird life includes ducks, nesting mergansers, osprey, bald eagles, shorebirds, phainopepla, red-winged blackbirds and great blue herons.

I have seen deer and javelina along the banks and found signs of beaver and river otters. During the late part of the season, this is a good section to jump hunt for ducks.

As the creek drops toward Horseshoe Canyon and Red Flat Draw it appears to flow directly up Horseshoe Canyon. Instead, it pools at the mouth of Horseshoe before abruptly turning north and plunging over a narrow rock bar, created by the outflow of Red Flat Draw and Horseshoe Canyon.

Here, all pretenses that this will simply be one more gorgeous stretch of Arizona riparian canyon are shattered. The creek had already been dropping at a rate of 25 feet per mile. For the next six miles that rate increases to 27 feet per mile. The canyon walls rush the river. The tops of the Redwall limestone cliffs reach 700 feet high and are, at times, within 0.2 of a mile of the creek.

The cliffs are eroded and stained red from a cap of sandstone. Caves, overhangs, window rocks, and balancing rocks appear as the Verde winds its way around Mormon Pocket. (This is also the general location of the lost gold mine mentioned in the Overview.)

It is possible to have visual overload. I've had winter days here when the combination of creek, red and white cliff walls, bald eagles, herons and snow was almost too beautiful to bear.

Come in the spring and scramble up the cliffs to find stands of cliff rose blooming. While on high, look down on the creek, shallow and clear, lined with mesquite, hackberry, walnut and the occasional cottonwood. Visit in the fall, when the leaves turn. In the summer you can refresh yourself at the springs that bubble to the surface a half-mile or so below Rafael Draw. In the winter, these same springs provide a welcome warm thermal offering to a cold traveler.

The creek becomes shallow and rock strewn as it fights its way down hill. It is a challenge for canoeists to find a way through the red stones and boulders. A beautiful and unboatable obstruction is located in the river where the railroad enters a short, curving tunnel. Large red rocks, from some distant landslide, have fallen from the cliffs to choke the river. This section can be portaged or the canoes manhandled through this section with care.

In high water this whole section becomes challenging. Increased water volume brings increased water velocity. The creek is narrow with lots of high water strainers and limited spaces to get out and scout.

The stream continues rocky with rock bars until the east side of Mormon Pocket, where it begins to gather in pools. This whole deep canyon is an important area for ducks, eagles and other wildlife.

> It doesn't matter if you are hiking, riding a horse, or canoeing. Don't rush this section. I have met people in here who were not having a good time. To a person, they had all badly over-estimated their ability to comfortably cover distance in this rugged land.

At the railroad tunnel (TRM 29) there are small limestone overhangs that are worth investigating. I've seen lots of bats here. There are a few good caves and deep overhangs throughout these parts, some high off the river.

After the creek turns to the south and travels down the east side of Mormon Pocket, it becomes peaceful. El Rio Verde then turns east and down a short, constricted drop into a lovely pool. This pool is created by a diversion dam that waters the private property that will shortly appear on the north side of the river.

Hunters, put away your guns! From now until you are past the mouth of Sycamore Canyon you are likely to be too close to some inhabited building to be able to legally shoot.

At about TRM 34.4 the Verde drops over a steep, shallow, heavy rapid and plows into the bank created by the railroad track. This rapid was created by the outwash of Railroad Draw. The rocks here are somewhat undercut, but the bank is definitely undercut.

The pools between the rocks at the bottom can be deep. The undercut bank has exposed tree roots waiting to snare a foolish high water boater. This rapid is runable. But it does require some cautions, especially if the water level is up and pushy.

The private property of the area known as Packard Ranch (Phelps Dodge owns most of the property) occupies river left to Sycamore Canyon. You will hit some fences, including some electric ribbon fences. The horses will stare at boaters as they pass, waiting for the opportunity to snicker at you as you work your way under the electric fence without touching it. (If you contact the fence, expect a mild, unpleasant shock.) You can't see them very well, but the Antelope Hills are emerging river right, away from the river.

Sycamore Creek signals a change in the canyon that holds the Verde. Suddenly and immediately on river left the limestone is replaced by black basalt, some 100 feet high. River right the limestone struggles for another mile before it succumbs to basalt also.

The flat area atop the cliffs on river left is known as Duff Flat. (Depending on what AGFD was able to arrange with Phelps Dodge, there may be a canoe access point here. Contact AGFD for details.)

Camping spots become rare. The talus slope from the basalt cliffs slant directly to the river, except at the apexes of some of the river bends and at a few other spots. The first of these very tight river turns also holds a small spring. About 1.5 miles below Sycamore Creek you will see a USGS river gauge river left.

Here, and at various other points along this basalt canyon (known as Box Canyon to the older locals) it is possible to access from above, river left. Duff Flats is crossed with roads, so folk drive to some point and they climb down a side drainage to the Verde. Unfortunately, along with some of these folk comes trash that doesn't make it out.

Near that gauging station another die is cast. Until now, the Verde had been flowing mostly to the east. Now it goes south. Except for a few stretches of useless rebellion, the Verde will hold to a southerly course until it enters the yards, faucets, and toilets of the Phoenix metro sprawl.

Another change occurs in this vicinity. Upstream from here the Verde is heavily dominated by native fish. AGFD surveys indicate that over 90 percent of the fish in the river upstream from here are natives. Not only are the fish native, there are lots of fish. The concentrations of fish life are extraordinarily heavy. Well, here it changes. The dominant fish species are now all exotic. In addition, the incidence of fish life drops pretty dramatically.

The creek below Sycamore consists of pools, separated by rapids. None of the rapids is above a Level Two. Most are short. (One long, rock-strewn rapid is shown on the topo maps.) Some, especially those on the bends, have larger rocks and require some maneuvering.

The basalt canyon slowly starts to melt into the Verde Valley—100 feet high, 80, 60, then 40 feet high, it sinks into the limestone that supports the Verde Valley. I've seen lots of quail in here, but hunting them is a challenge. When flushed, they fly to the top of the cliffs. Their flight pattern is predictable, but unusual. One shot per flock is all you get.

At SOB Canyon, TRM 42, you can get your first glimpse of the old smoke tower of TAPCO, journey's end. It plays hide-and-seek as you encounter increasing numbers of diversion dams, which foretell the fate awaiting the Verde. A mile or so from TAPCO, the canyon is gone. You move past sandy banks, a few old buildings, a few wrecked cars, and water pumps. The water pumps sit, like sleeping vampires, awaiting the heat to come and stimulate their thirsty need for the life force of the Verde.

A few bends and a large cottonwood bench appears on the left. It is private property, but presently open to the public. The ruins of TAPCO are across the river, sandwiched between the distant ruins of a cliff dwelling and the ruins at Tuzigoot. You and the Verde have come about 45 miles from Morgan Ranch.

Power Plants Along the Verde

On or near the Verde stand a number of abandoned or operating power plants. There is an abandoned, coal-fired plant near Clarkdale which is known as TAPCO. There is an operating, water-powered plant on the river at Childs, and another water-powered plant off the river, in the Fossil Creek drainage, at Irving.

The origin of all these plants is rooted in the early history of the electrification of Arizona. Near the turn of the century, the Arizona Power Company (TAPCO) provided power to the wired portions of Yavapai County.

TAPCO power plant ruins sit outside Clarkdale.
(Photo courtesy Arizona Public Service Company)

In 1897, Fossil Springs caught Anglo attention, especially since these springs cranked out 20,000 gallons of water per minute, day after day, season after season, year after year.

This water then rushed down a drop of 1,600 feet through Fossil Creek to reach the Verde. (The name "fossil" was given due to the high mineral content of the water. It tends to coat anything it flows over with minerals, making it appear to be fossilized.)

In 1907 the Arizona Power Company began construction on a hydro-powered plant at Childs. A seven-mile flume had to be constructed to imprison the springs and bring the water out of the Fossil Creek drainage.

All construction material, some of which had been manufactured in Germany, had to be hauled by mule train from the closest railhead at Mayer. Six hundred men, including many Yavapai Indians, and 450 mules labored for two years to build the plant. The water was brought to a point 1,075 feet above the site of the power plant and Stehr Lake was created to store the water. A pipe, which gradually decreases in diameter, was constructed to funnel the water down to the three generators below.

The plant at Irving was built just below the springs themselves 10 years later. It is smaller and has only one generator.

At one time these two small plants provided the electricity to Prescott, Jerome, Humboldt, the Verde Valley, in addition to the majority of the power for Phoenix. Because there are no ongoing costs for fuel, both plants are operated by Arizona Public Service Company to this very day. In 1986, the Childs plant was named a National Mechanical Engineering Landmark. It has also been named a National Historic Landmark.

The abandoned plant upriver from Clarkdale was built the same time as the Irving plant. Construction started in 1917 during World War I to provide power for increased activity at the copper mines. (War creates big demand for copper.) The plant was finished in 1918, just in time for peace. The demand for copper plummeted and by 1919 the plant had been mothballed.

In the 1920s the plant was run periodically solely to provide power to Phoenix at peak demand times. This practice continued until the 1960s when the plant was shut down for good. Now the ruins of past Indian culture overlooks one of the ruins of modern culture.

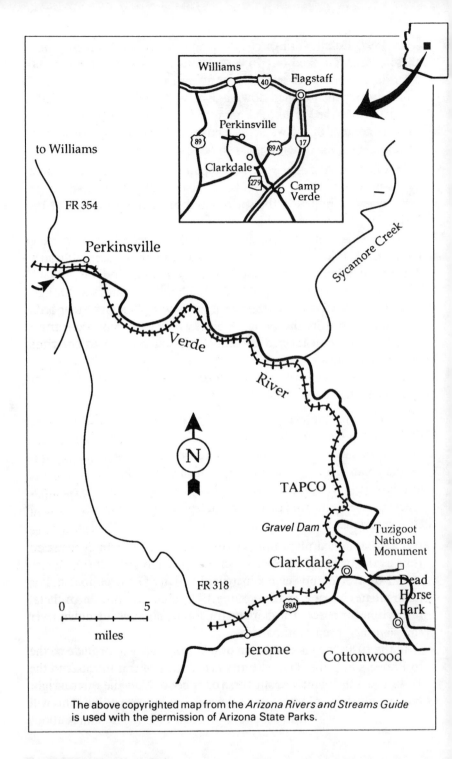

The above copyrighted map from the *Arizona Rivers and Streams Guide* is used with the permission of Arizona State Parks.

TAPCO to Dead Horse Park

Mileage: 6.5 miles

Elevation Change: 3400 to 3284

Warnings:
- Mill Tailings
- Private land
- Diversion Dams
- Cottonwood Ditch
- Gravel Pit

Motorized access:
- TAPCO. Cross the Tuzigoot bridge going toward Tuzigoot. Take the first left, which is FR 131. As you drop over the first hill, look for roads going into the cottonwood benches to the left of the road.
- Dead Horse Park
- Tuzigoot Bridge

Days for trip: one

This trip will never be popular with boaters, though I believe everyone in this state who uses water can benefit by traveling this segment at least once.

For a little bit below TAPCO things are OK. You see some nice cliffs. There are lots of cottonwood. And you get some fine views of the ruins at Tuzigoot Monument. All too quickly, you hit a huge black hill of mill tailings. Shortly after that you enter the pool created by the backwater of the Peck's Lake Diversion Dam.

This pool is a good place to try to spot birds and maybe to fish. It is not pretty. The dam is an amazing affair—a long curtain of metal sheeting, propped up (no lie) by large posts sunk on the down river side.

It is pretty easy to get a canoe over this obstruction. Paddle to the right side and climb up on the earthen works. Line your boat to the edge of the dam, which is only three or four feet high on the river right side. Pull up on your bowline and forward on your stern line. This will cause your canoe to move forward until the edge of the dam is about midway down the bottom. Next, pull up on your sternline and your canoe will slide over until the bow hits the creek bottom below. Climb down, finish manhandling your boat into the creek below, and paddle away.

> **Do not approach this dam at high water. Being swept over could result in serious injuries.**

The dam provides about eight feet of head. One of the better ideas I have heard bounced around the Verde Valley is to apply for SLIF (State Lake Improvement Funds) and use this head to create an artificial whitewater course. Properly constructed, that eight foot could be converted into 50 yards or so of solid Class 2 whitewater. Where such runs have been created elsewhere, they have proven to be a commercial draw, in addition to providing recreation for the local community.

Below the dam the creek flows under Tuzigoot Bridge. River left is part of the Verde Greenbelt. River right is private land. Shortly you drop over the diversion dam that provides water for Dead Horse Park.

Below this diversion dam the river quickens its pace and heads into a narrow chute. Cottonwoods start to close in and the scene promises to be very pretty. There is a sense of relief, after the last couple miles of river where humankind's damaging impact has been all too obvious. The idea of paddling a narrow run through a canopy of cottonwoods is exciting.

As you enter the narrow chute, your eyes are naturally drawn to the tops of the high cottonwoods. This particular habitat is critically important to a huge variety of birds. It is comforting and reassuring to see it here in good health.

Ahead you see the now quite-narrow creek makes a sharp right turn. You round the turn and stare at a large metal water gate. Gotcha! The river is gone. You are paddling in the Cottonwood Ditch.

Beach your boat river left and drag it out of the ditch. See that marsh on the left? The one with virtually no water? That is what is left of the Verde River. Forty-nine miles below its perennial birthplace, the Verde almost dies. Up to 80 percent of all the water that enters the Verde Valley disappears into this ditch.

Drag your boat over to the marsh and walk back upstream on river left. Go back to the point where you first noticed the creek seeming to narrow, and look at your feet. This weed-covered bank is an old diversion dam. Once on it you can see the unnatural regular patterns in the order of the rocks. Originally, the creek turned left here.

Return to your boat and drag it down the old creek bed. The large river cobbles here have not yet learned that the river is gone. As you walk, notice this creek, the Verde River, gathering more water as it struggles to recover. There is less water here than at its birthplace near Morgan Ranch.

Over the next couple hundred yards, a thin, thin stream of water moves around the river cobbles which were rubbed round by the flowing waters that now grow lawns in Cottonwood.

Walk a little further to where the river turns right and the irrigation ditch from Dead Horse and Tuzigoot re-enters. There is a substantial little marsh here. Unless the river is higher than normal, the water will be clear for the first time in miles. The water works its way through reeds and the sediment is filtered by the plants. The combined views of marsh and distant Black Hills are wonderful.

As the marsh ends, a gravel pit appears on the left. The gravel pits along the river in the Verde Valley have been the subject of controversy, court cases, Environmental Protection Agency (EPA) action. The controversy with this particular pit has included violence involving firearms.

Travel around the next bend to the left and you will be at the low water crossing that leads into Dead Horse State Park. This park is worth a visit.

You, and El Rio de Los Reyes, are about 52 miles below Morgan Ranch.

Sedge grass can grow as thick as a carpet.

Green-winged Teal. (Reprinted from *Arizona Game Birds* by David Brown, artist Paul Bosman, The University of Arizona Press, ©1989. Courtesy The U of A Press.)

Wood Ducks. (Reprinted from *Arizona Game Birds* by David Brown, artist Paul Bosman, The University of Arizona Press, ©1989. Courtesy The U of A Press.)

Birds

Here are birds that I have comonly seen along with a few that you may not see but will definitely be worth an "Oh, wow!" if you do.

Red-Tail Hawk

One of the first raptors people learn to identify.

Black Hawk

Considered rare. However, you have a good chance of seeing one along the Verde and certain of its tributaries. Black Hawks nest along the Verde and its tribs. They hunt toads, crayfish and similar prey. They have two white bands on their tails and yellow, dangling legs.

Golden Eagle

You may see these large predators along the creek but what may appear to be a golden eagle is more likely to be an immature bald eagle.

Bald Eagles

During the winter, Arizona receives bald eagles migrating down from northern climates. We also have our own resident nesting population. Bald eagles prey on fish but will also take waterfowl.

We do not get breeding eagles here from elsewhere. Only an eagle which was hatched here will breed here. A nesting eagle agitated by rude humans will fly in circles and make noises similar to the calls of gulls. The egg will often die if left uncovered for 15 minutes or longer. Disturbing the nest violates the Bald Eagle Protection Act, Migratory Bird Treaty, Endangered Species Act, and Forest Service rules for breaking a federal closure rule. Fines are heavy and jail time is possible. Many sites are monitored by nestwatchers with high powered optics and radios to use to contact law enforcement officials.

At least two new nests were located since this book was first published in 1990. You should assume that there are nests and federal closures not listed in this book. Closure boundaries and closure dates are subject to change. The only truly up-to-date source is the office of the Forest Service which manages the section of creek you expect to travel. With that said, here are the boundaries of the areas closed to land access, or stopping by boaters, of which I was aware at the time of this writing. I've listed them by river section. These closures are all seasonal, running about from the first of January through June.

Perkinsville to Tapco

Perkinsville— Do not camp on private land. If a closure is in effect it will start near the bridge and end a couple of miles downstream.

Camp Verde to Beasley Flats

West Clear Creek—When the closure is in effect you will encounter a sign announcing the closure about a mile upriver of West Clear Creek and a sign downriver (between 1/2 mile and one mile) announcing the end of the closure.

Beasley Flat to Childs

Falls—The closure typically starts at the Falls and ends at the mouth of Sycamore Creek #2.

Brown Spring—You may encounter closures starting near or up river of Gap Creek and ending below Cold Water Creek. There is a suspected alternate net in the area.

Childs to Horseshoe Dam

East Verde—If a closure exists, it will start somewhere below Nasty Little Dogleg rapid and end somewhere above the mouth of the East Verde.

Table Mountain—This closure will likely start at Mule Shoe and end before the end of Mule Shoe. This is a watched nest as it has been purposefully disturbed.

Horseshoe Lake—If a restriction exists it will start below Sheep Bridge somewhere and end near the start of the lake.

Bartlett Dam to the Salt River

Bartlett Dam—This closure **to all entry** starts below the dam near the gauging station and ends somewhere below Bootleg Canyon.

Fort McDowell—Look for signs the entire time you are paddling past reservation land. If a closure exists, it will probably be signed.

Osprey

I've seen these fish hawks mostly in the Perkinsville stretch. They seem to go elsewhere when the bald eagles arrive.

While doing fish population surveys with the Arizona Game and Fish Department, we have found fish which carry scars from where some taloned aerial predator struck and almost caught dinner. No one knows how many of the fish so wounded die. It is clear that at least some recover. We find some fish damaged by herons, also.

Canada Geese. (Reprinted from Arizona Game Birds by David Brown, artist Paul Bosman, The University of Arizona Press, ©1989. Courtesy The U of A Press.)

Falcons

If you see a falcon in a canyon area, there is a good chance that it is a peregrine. However, it could also be a harrier or a prairie falcon.

Common Loon

Every once in a while one of these will show up at Peck's Lake or Horseshoe Lake.

Canada Geese

These beautiful, and tasty, birds visit the Verde in small numbers in the dead of winter. You are most likely to find them in the Wilderness section below Childs.

Mallards and Teals

Very common along the entire Verde during the winter.

Phainopepla

Sometimes called a black cardinal. This beautiful black bird with white wing patches is common along the Verde. Its soft, short whistle is regularly heard.

Great Blue Heron

Extremely common along the Verde. This majestic fish hunter nests along the Verde in large rookeries (typically, some large cottonwood) shared by many herons. I have been able to see twenty or more herons in a large rookery in the upper reaches of the Verde. Their croaking squawks and large wing span make me think of pterodactyls.

Green Heron

Look for these small relatives of the great blue throughout the Verde Valley.

Common Mergansers. (Reprinted from *Arizona Game Birds* by David Brown, artist Paul Bosman, The University of Arizona Press, ©1989. Courtesy The U of A Press.)

Common Mergansers

These fish-eating ducks do nest along the Verde River. During the spring, you can see females with their ducklings. Nesting mergansers seem absent along the Salt River, or at least, they are not present in the numbers found along the Verde. One wildlife biologist has suggested that the heavy boater traffic along the Salt during the spring causes the family group to be broken up as the female and brood attempt to flee the intrusive boaters. The isolated and lost ducklings are easy pickings for a wide variety of predators.

From my own experience on the Verde, I know that the female and young will flee downstream for considerable distances in front of large boats (rafts), boats that are moving quickly, or otherwise act as if they have predation in mind. I also know from personal experience that it is possible for a boater to paddle **quietly** and **SLOWLY** past such a family group. The key elements seem to be keeping as much distance as possible, not paddling directly toward the birds, and moving slowly and quietly.

Kingfishers

The belted kingfisher is the most commonly seen of aerial hunters that dive from the air into the water after fish.

Cliff Swallows and Bank Swallows

I have seen both along the Verde and its tribs, but cliff swallows are more common. Here is another example where boaters need to show some respect for wildlife's need for privacy while raising young. Boaters who paddle too close to the mud nests not only throw the parents into panic, but at times, the older chicks will abandon the nest in fear, exposing them to the much greater risks which exist outside those small mud walls.

Snipes, Sandpipers and Dippers

These shorebirds can all be found in the Verde watershed.

Gambel's Quail. (Reprinted from *Arizona Game Birds* by David Brown, artist Paul Bosman, The University of Arizona Press, ©1989. Courtesy The U of A Press.)

Mourning Dove. (Reprinted from *Arizona Game Birds* by David Brown, artist Paul Bosman, The University of Arizona Press, ©1989. Courtesy The U of A Press.)

Mourning Doves and Gambel's Quail

Both are common small game birds along the Verde.

Flycatchers, Phoebes, Wrens, Tanagers, Sparrows

These, and other insect eaters, are present in large numbers.

Roadrunners

Hunter of lizards, snakes and other small critters, including birds.

Wood Ducks

Give a cheer if you are fortunate to see these colorful waterfowl.

Dead Horse Park to Bridgeport

Mileage: 4.5 miles

Elevation Change: 3284 to 3260

Warnings:
- Downed trees
- Gravel pits
- Private land

Motorized access:
- Dead Horse Park
- Bridgeport, where RT 89A crosses the Verde.

Days for trip: one

Dead Horse State Park is worth some time. It has good camping and picnic facilities and offers pond or stream fishing. The rangers can usually provide information about the river, including information important to river runners. It is the site of Verde River Day, usually held in the late summer or early fall. The attractive nature of this park is reflected in the fact that they receive over 50,000 visitors a year.

It is possible to canoe from Dead Horse to Bridgeport in a matter of hours, but why hurry? There is bass in these waters and, in the winter, stocked trout. When I'm fishing, I can spend all day on this segment. In the fall, you can admire the reflection of golden-leaved cottonwoods in the water. At any time of year, you can appreciate intimate little pools. At any time of year you can also see the devastation left by poorly-regulated gravel pits.

The first mile or so is lovely. Cottonwood benches harbor lots of bird life. The stream is often shallow, still recovering from the theft of the waters at Cottonwood Ditch, a scant couple miles upstream. There are some deeper pools, and some nice views of the Black Hills.

Then you hit a gravel pit. Notice the piles of barren rock. Notice the bombed stream bed. Notice the dead cottonwoods.

After exiting the war zone, the river turns south. You pass through riparian zones with limestone bluffs off the river left. This is important bird habitat. There are unobtrusive homes and close trees. Watch for signs of beaver.

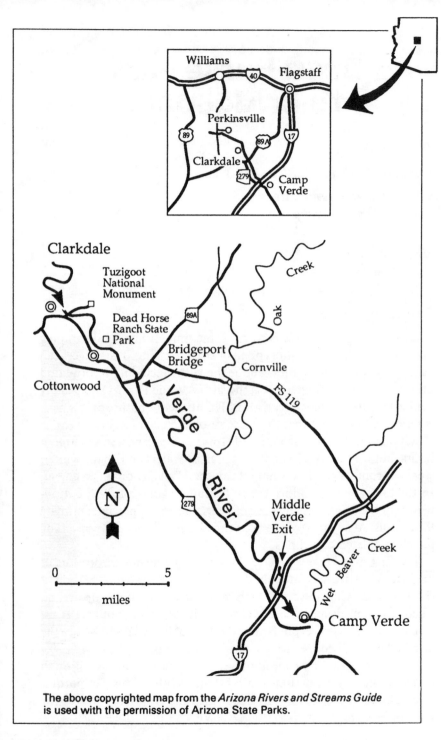

The above copyrighted map from the *Arizona Rivers and Streams Guide* is used with the permission of Arizona State Parks.

Bridgeport, where RT 89A crosses the Verde, is an excellent river access point. The land underneath the bridge is public, lots of available parking, restaurants and a bar.

This section is often very shallow. If I'm going here, I try to go with a light canoe. You will enjoy this section most at cfs levels above readings of 100 at the Camp Verde gauge. It is worth your time to boat this. Many of the canoeists I have met in the area like this segment because of the easy access at Dead Horse and Bridgeport.

At Bridgeport, the Verde has traveled about 56.5 miles since its perennial birth.

Where man does not interfere,
riparian growth hugs the Verde quite close.

Common Cattail. (Reprinted from *Illustrated Guide of Arizona Weeds* by Kittie Parker, artist Lucretia Breazeale Hamilton, The University of Arizona Press, ©1972. Courtesy The U of A Press.)

Seepwillow Baccharis. (Reprinted from *Illustrated Guide of Arizona Weeds* by Kittie Parker, artist Lucretia Breazeale Hamilton, The University of Arizona Press, ©1972. Courtesy The U of A Press.)

Western or Netleaf Hackberry. reprinted from *Trees and Shrubs of the Southwest Desert* by Lyman Benson and Robert A. Darrow, artist Lucretia Breazeale Hamilton, The University of Arizona Press, ©1981. Courtesy The U of A Press.)

Plants

There are lots of them out there. I started to put together a halfway adequate list and it threatened to envelop the book.

Sunflowers

There are a variety of sunflowers which grow in Arizona, most of them (but not all) yellow. Included in this large family are desert-marigolds, brittlebush, blanketflower, goldfields, and blackfoot daisies. The large flowers I saw along the upper Verde near Morgan Ranch were a sunflower.

Sunflower. (Reprinted from *Illustrated Guide of Arizona Weeds* by Kittie Parker, artist Lucretia Breazeale Hamilton, The University of Arizona Press, ©1972. Courtesy The U of A Press.)

Chuparosa

This shrub produces red, tubular flowers in the spring, attracting lots of hummingbirds.

Beardtongue

Hummingbirds are also attracted to this red member of the snapdragon family. It is common along the East Verde and Sycamore Creeks #3 and #4.

Sacred Datura

This jimpson weed is a member of the nightshade family. There is no missing or mistaking its large, white, trumpet flowers. The flowers are pollenated by bees and hawkmoths. **All parts of the plant are poisonous!**

Sacred Datura. (Reprinted from *Illustrated Guide of Arizona Weeds* by Kittie Parker, artist Lucretia Breazeale Hamilton, The University of Arizona Press, ©1972. Courtesy The U of A Press.)

Coyote Gourd

This gourd-producing vine bears large yellow flowers. There is a coyote gourd of frightening size at one of the springs below Rafael Draw.

Desert Rose Mallow

These large, mostly white flowers atop a sick-looking shrub can be seen along the Verde above King Canyon.

Strawberry Hedgehog and Pincushion Cactus

These two different cactus will at times take root in small outcroppings on creek side cliffs. When in bloom, the contrast of rock and plant is a special visual gift.

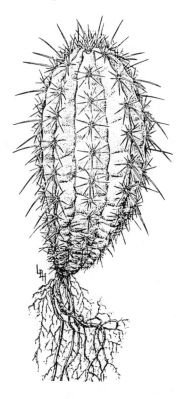

Hedgehog Cactus. (Reprinted from *Cacti of Arizona* by Lyman Benson, artist Lucretia Breazeale Hamilton, The University of Arizona Press, ©1981. Courtesy The U of A Press.)

Desert Ironwood. (Reprinted from *Trees and Shrubs of the Southwest Desert* by Lyman Benson and Robert A Darrow, artist Lucretia Breazeal Hamilton, The University of Arizona Press, ©1981. Courtesy The U of Press.)

Ironwood

The soft, lavender pastel of the flowers of this desert tree follow the early summer yellow blooms of the palo verde.

Reeds

The very large reeds seen below Childs are bullrushes. They provide important habitat for numerous birds. Redwinged blackbirds seem particularly attracted to them. The smaller reeds which border the upper section of the Verde are sedge grass of some sort. Sedge grass grows to about knee high and can be as thick as a lawn. Cattails grow sporadically from the Verde Valley down river.

Algae

A variety of algae grows in the streams of the Verde watershed where it provides food and shelter to denizens of the water, land and air.

Duckweed

The smallest blooming plant. These tiny dots of green are thick in the waters below the Morgan Ranch.

Watercress

A noticeable round-leafed plant growing from the bottom of the stream. It is edible.

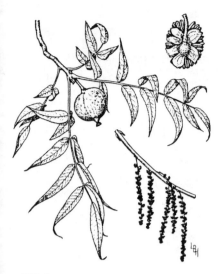

Arizona Black Walnut. (Reprinted from *Trees and Shrubs of the Southwest Desert* by Lyman Benson and Robert A. Darrow, artist Lucretia Breazeale Hamilton, The University of Arizona Press, ©1981. Courtesy The U of A Press.)

Walnut

The walnut tree is common along the Verde above Clarkdale. Below Clarkdale it is most often found along the tributaries to the Verde.

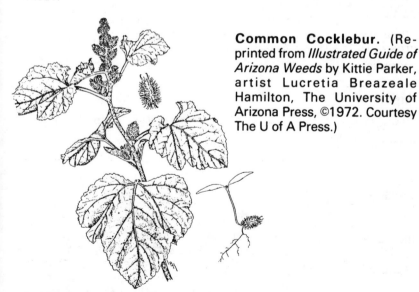

Common Cocklebur. (Reprinted from *Illustrated Guide of Arizona Weeds* by Kittie Parker, artist Lucretia Breazeale Hamilton, The University of Arizona Press, ©1972. Courtesy The U of A Press.)

Cocklebur

Enemy of all canines. I took a dog on a river trip in the fall once that came back looking so bad, I probably could have had him named a federal disaster area.

Sycamore

Does the fact that four tributaries to the Verde are named after this tree give you a hint as to how common it is? They are great trees. I believe the best specimens are found on Beaver Creek below Montezuma Castle.

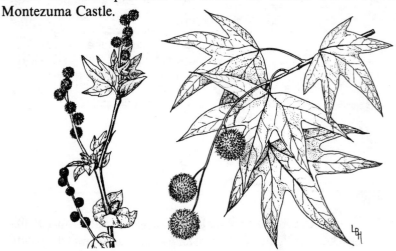

Sycamore. (Reprinted from *Trees and Shrubs of the Southwest Desert* by Lyman Benson and Robert A. Darrow, artist Lucretia Breazeale Hamilton, The University of Arizona Press, ©1981. Courtesy The U of A Press.)

Trumpet Flower

This shrub or small tree bears yellow flowers. Common along sections of the Verde.

Yellow Trumpet Flower. (Reprinted from *Trees and Shrubs of the Southwest Desert* by Lyman Benson and Robert A. Darrow, artist Lucretia Breazeale Hamilton, The University of Arizona Press, ©1981. Courtesy The U of A Press.)

Saltcedar. (Reprinted from *Illustrated Guide of Arizona Weeds* by Kittie Parker, artist Lucretia Breazeale Hamilton, The University of Arizona Press, ©1972. Courtesy The U of A Press.)

Salt Cedar, Tamarisk

This foul invader and invasive plant will take over the banks of any creek that can't fight back. It is most often found below dams, where the river is emasculated. It occurs along the Verde above Horseshoe Lake, but it is not common, until you get below the dam.

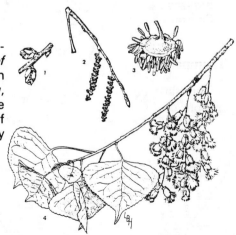

Fremont Cottonwood. (Reprinted from *Trees and Shrubs of the Southwest Desert* by Lyman Benson and Robert A. Darrow, artist Lucretia Breazeale Hamilton, The University of Arizona Press, ©1981. Courtesy The U of A Press.)

Cottonwoods

At one time, these beautiful and inspiring trees were targeted for elimination by a water company for the Phoenix area. These native plants were using water which could have been used instead by people downstream. Such vegetation control projects are not dead. As I write, one is being considered for the upland portion of the Verde and Salt watersheds.

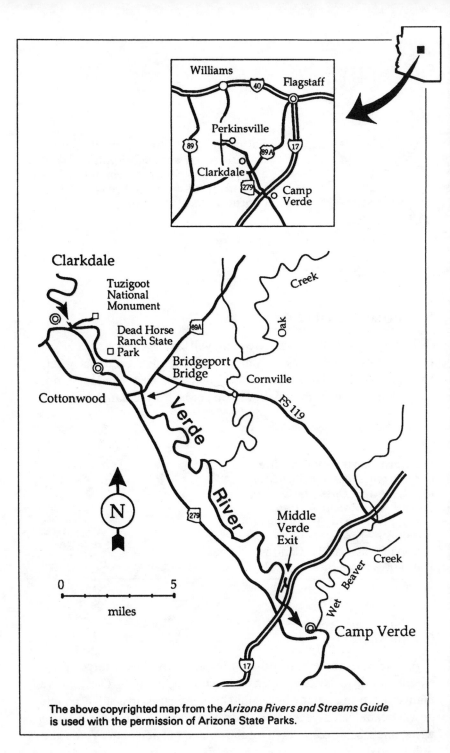

The above copyrighted map from the *Arizona Rivers and Streams Guide* is used with the permission of Arizona State Parks.

Bridgeport to Oak Creek

Mileage: 8 miles

Elevation Change: 3260 to 3180

Warnings: ● Private land
        ● Gravel operations
        ● Diversion dam

Motorized access:

- Bridgeport, where RT 89A crosses the Verde.
- Black Canyon (ask for directions, locally).
- Bignott Beach. Follow signs off road into Thousand Trails.
- Thousand Trails Campground. Turnoff is located off RT 89 between Cottonwood and Camp Verde. Access is either by foot from public parking lot near campground or by four-wheel drive roads accessed at a turnoff just prior to Thousand Trails labeled "Sheep Crossing."

Days needed: One to two

This is a great stretch, particularly suitable for beginning boaters, or for trips with children. It offers nice views, intimate little spots, camping as well as opportunities to fish and swim. Much of the land is privately owned, so non-boaters may find access difficult.

At normal water flows, this section has no unusual dangers. Trees can always fall into the creek, so boaters must always be on the lookout for strainers. However, the current is typically slow, so there is no need for any boaters who show sense to find themselves in trouble.

The first four miles show intimate pools and riffles. Many of these are contained by banks covered with trees, brush or the creek bouncing up against limestone cliffs of various heights. About four miles into the trip, the land to the river left becomes flat and open. It stays that way until you near the mouth of Oak Creek. River right keeps some uplift the entire way through this section.

Black Canyon and Wilbur Canyon join the river about five miles below Bridgeport. Black Canyon is easy to spot, if you know what to look for, or if you have been following your course on a topo mat. Here you can find huge cottonwoods and public land. The Forest Service plans to develop this river access point over the next few years.

It is possible to drive into this area, as the mounds of trash left by Driving Destroyers indicate. However, being able to drive in does not mean there is a paved road. It is possible to access Black Canyon off the Cottonwood-Camp Verde road. Then, you drive down the wash.

Black Canyon is only a couple of miles above Oak Creek. Were you to take one day to canoe to Black Canyon, you could easily make Oak Creek early the next morning. (Take some extra trash out with you.) As you approach Oak Creek, the creek gains some midstream rocks and some more trees close on the bank. River left gains some height, as it moves to create the limestone cliffs found at and just below Oak Creek.

Bignott Beach, a quarter-mile above Oak Creek provides motorized access which will also be improved by the Forest Service over the next few years. If you have such a vehicle, you can also get down to the river below Thousand Trails and take out there at the mouth of Oak Creek at Sheeps Crossing.

The area below Thousand Trails is in the flood plain. The land alternates stony and sandy with heavy growths of riparian vegetation. You could park in the public parking area to the side of Thousand Trails and carry your gear up to your vehicle. Perhaps the best solution would be to call one of the outfitters mentioned in the book for the Verde Valley area and arrange for them to pick you up and shuttle you out.

The White Hills start appearing river left as you approach Oak Creek. They look across the creek at the much larger Black Hills.

It is possible to combine the section just above this one with this one to create a longer trip. At 100 cfs (Camp Verde) I left Dead Horse at 1 p.m. and pulled into Black Canyon at 5 p.m., paddling straight through.

I always caution folk against biting off too much distance. There is nothing wrong with taking your time down the river, having fun and sight seeing instead of making time. However, it should be reasonable for marginally competent boaters to make it from Dead Horse to Black Canyon (10 miles) in one full day of paddling.

This is a particularly nice section. It offers fishing, swimming, camping, good views, is easily accessible, and is serviced by canoe rental businesses. All we need do is protect it.

When it reaches the confluence with Oak Creek, the Verde has been a living, perennial stream for about 64 miles.

Stream bank reeds provide important habitat for animal life.

Father, son and dog paddle into a Verde evening.

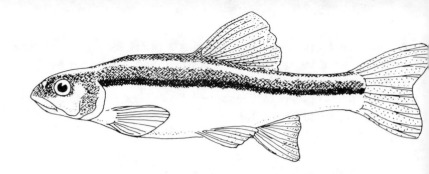

Long Fin Dace (Courtesy Arizona Game and Fish Department. Artist: Randy Babb)

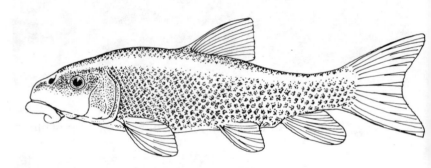

Desert Sucker, also known as **Gila Sucker** (Courtesy Arizona Game and Fish Department. Artist: Randy Babb)

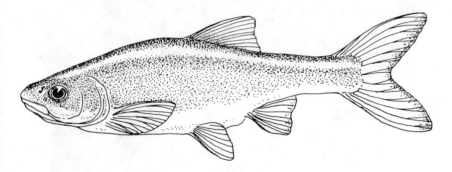

Roundtail Chub (Courtesy Arizona Game and Fish Department. Artist: Randy Babb)

Fish

Let's start off by dividing the fish of the Verde into two categories. "Natives," the species which existed here prior to the coming of Europeans, and "exotics," which were introduced to the region by those of European descent.

Natives

Spikedace Minnow

This little critter has very small scales and sits on the Federal Threatened and Endangered Species list. Its population varies widely though numbers do seem to go up when there are not many floods. This wonderful animal is presently helping to protect the Verde by its mere existence. Federal laws prohibit withdrawing so much water from the Verde that the habitat of the fish would be destroyed. Speckled and Long Fin Dace also swim the Verde.

Desert Sucker/Mountain Sucker

These are two different species. AFGD biologists have pointed out the difference to me a number of times. The mouth of the Mountain Sucker faces the creek bottom. When you look at the fish head on, you see nose, not mouth. When you look at the Desert Sucker head on, the mouth is clearly visible. Both species can grow to over a foot long. The Mountain Sucker is also called the Gila Mountain Sucker. The Desert Sucker is also known as the Gila Sucker.

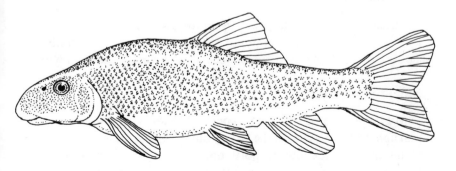

Gila Mountain Sucker, also known as **Mountain Sucker** (Courtesy Arizona Game and Fish Department. Artist: Randy Babb)

Razorback Suckers

A Federal T & E species. At present, AGFD is trying to re-establish these fish into the Verde River by stocking hatchery-raised fish.

Gila Chub

A candidate for T & E status on the state list. These fish are common in the upper Verde. They grow to over a foot in length, and will hit flies and lures. In my experience, they hit very hard, but give up the fight quickly.

Squawfish

At one time, these fish abounded in our streams. Before the dams were built, Squawfish weighing over 80 pounds were pitchforked out of the Salt River in Phoenix and used for fertilizer. No longer. AGFD is trying to re-establish these in the Verde also, but with limited effect. Squawfish eat each other, so it is hard to economically raise them in a hatchery. All stocking attempts have been made by using lots of small, inexperienced fry, much to the joy and gratitude of hungry predators all along the upper Verde.

Exotics

Largemouth Bass

These popular fighting (and eating) fish are found along the entire length of the Verde in spotty populations, never in any great numbers. Those populations that do exist occur away from the deep canyons.

Smallmouth Bass

My favorite game fish. These spunky fish are a joy on the end of a real light test line. As with the largemouths, "bronzebacks" are found all along the Verde, but in spotty populations. The populations can be, and often are, quite large, but they are spotty in location. For example, there are consistent populations of smallmouths above the Perkinsville Canyon, though not so many in the canyon below US

Mines. There are virtually no smallmouths in the Perkinsville Canyon.

From the Verde Valley down to the Salt, smallmouths can always be found somewhere. I have had my best luck in the Wild and Scenic section, but that is also where I fish the most. Other anglers I have talked to mention good action in the Verde Valley, especially from Dead Horse Park to just past Oak Creek. I'm willing to bet there are good populations in the Camp Verde area also, especially in the marshy-edged stuff. Many of the smallmouths pulled from the Verde will show a strong red color around their eyes. This can result from a number of reasons, the most likely one being stress. Research has shown that smallmouths will move great distances, miles and miles, in order to find conditions to their liking.

Carp

Introduced as food fish. They are very good eating once you figure out how to deal with the bones. They do not do the aerial acrobatics of a smallmouth, but they are a strong fish and put up quite an underwater fight. They are common all along the Verde.

Catfish (Channel, Bullheads, Flatheads)

Found throughout the Verde. The heaviest concentrations are found starting at the Verde Valley. The section near Camp Verde has a reputation of good catfishing, as does the remainder of the stream to the Salt. Twenty-pound cats have been caught at Red Creek. The Verde below Horseshoe is known for growing big cats. Most of the cats I've taken have been 12 to 20 inches long. They are my favorite eating fish. I canoe with a dutch oven just for these gems.

Green Sunfish

Present, but not in real large numbers.

Trout

Stocked into Oak Creek, West Clear Creek and, during the winter, the Verde. Healthy populations exist in Wet Beaver Creek and West Clear Creek. Our native trout, long since driven from the Verde, have been re-established in Gap Creek.

Mosquitofish

A small minnow dumped into waters all over the state to help keep our massive mosquito population at bay. The impact was to drive our native top minnows to the brink of extinction.

Red Shiners

A common bait minnow. Found in large numbers all through the Verde. They compete with spikedace.

One of the puzzles occupying AGFD personnel is why exotics don't do well in the deep canyon. Prevailing thought, at least prevailing around the campfire, is that since exotics did not evolve in canyons beset by flashfloods, they don't know how to deal with them. They either get washed down stream, or stranded along the banks when the waters recede. It makes sense to me. If I canoe a stretch of canyon after a flood, the dried backwaters are littered with the skeletons of carp, bass and catfish, but not the skeletons of suckers.

All of these river fish, game and nongame, exotics and natives, are tracked by biologists using a variety of techniques. To gain access, they use rafts and canoes. Rafts are used only at the high flows. Most of the time, the rivers are surveyed using canoes. Seine nets, pole nets and generators are loaded along with all required camping gear into the canoe.

Electro-fishing is done to survey larger fish (not minnows) that are found near the surface of the water. Electro-fishing is inefficient below about six feet of water. Current is run through the water, with the positive terminal off the bow and the negative off the stern. The shock stuns the fish for a matter of seconds. During those brief seconds, the biologists net as many as possible and put them into a live well.

Once on shore, the fish are weighed, measured, cleaned of parasites, tagged and returned to the water. Almost all the fish recover completely within five minutes. A small percentage die, usually because they came in contact with the cable delivering the positive charge. Trout seem the most susceptible to fatalities.

Tagged fish are followed either by their being recaught on future survey trips, or because the fish was caught by some angler who does the right thing and calls the Department to report the tag numbers. For those of you who are interested, and I'm sure there are some, the current is pulsed D.C. current. The pulse frequency is 80 pulses per second with a 40 percent width. Between three and four amps are used and about 300 volts.

Coffelt Manufacturing, based in Flagstaff, has developed a system of electrofishing which appears to lower the fatality rate of the fish. They use a lower pulse frequency per second (15 to 60) and a narrow pulse width (25 percent). The canoe based electro-fishing surveys done on the Verde have discovered that many of the native fish in the Verde, especially those whose numbers have plummeted, are infested with the parasite *Lernaea cyprinacea*. The population of this little wormlike critter, which attaches to the skin of the fish, is known to have exploded in Verde waters between the 1930's and the 1960's. Fish infested with this parasite tend to low body weight and tend to die quickly when stressed, indicating that they are already under some stress.

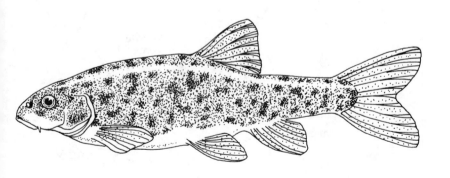

Speckled Dace (Courtesy Arizona Game and Fish Department. Artist: Randy Babb)

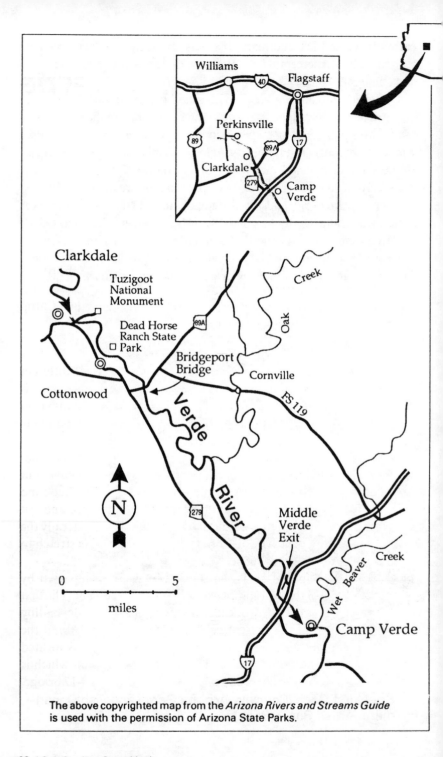

The above copyrighted map from the *Arizona Rivers and Streams Guide* is used with the permission of Arizona State Parks.

Oak Creek to Camp Verde

Mileage: 12 miles

Elevation Change: 3180 to 3080

Warnings:
- Ugly, dangerous diversion dams
- Two gravel pits
- Private land
- Reservation land

Motorized access:
- Bignott Beach. Take turn to Thousand Trails and then follow sign to Bignott Beach.
- Camp Verde. At the bridge where the Middle Verde—Camp Verde road (FR 646) crosses the Verde River.

Days needed: One to two

This stretch is difficult to describe. It has a number of different experiences within it, some good and some bad. Overall, this section is characterized by low banks on river left, with some very distant views of the White Hills. The land is dry and there are often a good many cattle.

River right has a little more in the way of elevation and sometimes offers grey/white cliffs. The current moves along at a regular but moderate pace. There are only a couple of rapids, at Cherry Creek and I-17. There is noticeably less vegetation here than the sections above it or below it. Some houses are visible and some trash, but generally the creek has a feeling of rural isolation. It would not be a fun stretch to paddle if you had a headwind.

There are a couple of areas that have been heavily impacted by gravel pits. Each of these pits impacts about one mile of river. The first one you encounter may be working right up to the water, depending on the resolution of the present conflict between the EPA and the gravel companies that operate along the Verde. This pit is located about one-and-a-half miles below the OK Diversion Dam which is near Thousand Trails. The second pit is located below the I-17 bridge, which is a little more than nine miles into your trip.

There are two diversion dams I want to call to your attention—Eureka Dam which is four miles below the OK Dam and the Woods Ditch Dam which is about five miles below the OK Dam.

The open land does have a rural feel to it and there is a very interesting island at the Cloverleaf Ranch. (This island does not show on the topo maps). River left seems to be the older of the river passages. It is overhung with trees and could easily acquire a strainer from one trip to the next.

When I paddled through here there was a clear passage. The creek was filled with a growth of algae that parted like flowing hair as I floated through. One quiet shady backwater held untold numbers of water striders, the first water insect I learned to identify when a child and still one of my very favorites to see.

Below the second gravel pit, the edges of the creek take on a marshy nature. Cattails appear and some reeds. Just above I-17, and then below the second gravel pit, cottonwood benches rejoin the river and it again becomes a riparian zone.

I did see fishermen all along this section (I had headwinds so I didn't fish) fishing in the gravel pits themselves. In fact, squawfish, once eliminated from the Verde, was caught on a hook and line in one of these gravel pits.

Below the Cloverleaf Ranch you paddle on and off reservation land. Unless you are a member of the Yavapai Tribe, this means you are **a visitor on private land.**

There is an interesting little rapid immediately underneath the I-17 bridge. I enjoyed my drop down through it and would like to paddle it at higher flows.

Finally, as you near Camp Verde, the Black Hills again become visible. Near the end of your trip you will pass below Grief Hill, which was the site of armed conflict between Indians and settlers back in the early days.

Take out is at Camp Verde, where the road from Middle Verde enters Camp Verde. You and the Verde have traveled 76 miles from Morgan Ranch.

Mammals

Livestock (cattle/horses)

Depending on the grazing patterns at any given point in time, you could see livestock anywhere along the Verde except the urbanized sections. Sometimes they add color. Sometimes they simply leave feces and urine all over the best campsites.

Mule Deer

If the deer you see has a white rump which is visible while the tail is down, you are looking at a mule deer, not a whitetail. In addition, look for long ears. The antlers differ from those of a whitetail, also. Bucks lose their antlers near the end of January. You could see mule deer anywhere along the Verde. In fact, any deer you do see is probably a mule deer.

I have seen mule deer in the Perkinsville section, the basalt box canyon, and all along the river below Beasley Flats and above Horseshoe.

Whitetails

Small, intelligent deer of the canyons and higher elevations. They have brown rumps and white under their tails. They raise their tails and display it as a sign of alarm, an act called "flagging." It is possible, but unlikely, that you would see one along the Verde. Bucks lose their antlers a month or so later than mule deer.

Black Bears

Black bears are spotted along the Verde mostly when prickly pear fruit is ripe. Your best chance of sighting (and even it is not too good) is in the Wild and Scenic portion.

River Otters

These are imports from Louisiana, introduced by AGFD to replace the native population, thought to be extinct. There are not many. It is conceivable you might see them anywhere below Verde Ranch and above Horseshoe Lake. I have seen otters below Verde Ranch and at Cottonwood Basin, below Beasley Flats. I have seen fecal signposts of otters in the Perkinsville canyon and in the Wild and Scenic stretch. I have seen their tracks at Verde Falls.

These predators eat mostly fish. One way to help identify their feces is that otter feces are usually nothing but fish scales with, perhaps, a crayfish thrown in.

Beaver

Beaver are common along virtually the entire Verde and many of the tributaries, such as Oak Creek, Beaver Creek and Wet Beaver Creek. Beaver dams can be found on the Verde above Perkinsville and on Wet Beaver Creek. I've not seen a lodge anywhere. The beaver apparently den in the river banks. Beaver-gnawed trees are a common sight.

Beaver are shy and nocturnal. You are not likely to see one. On the upper Verde, it appears the pools behind the dams help create a favorable habitat for a number of species of native fish. I have seen beaver on private land high on the Verde and heard the slap of their tails as far down as Railroad Draw. I have on occasion seen their sign down to Horseshoe.

Javelina

Common all along the Verde. These animals are virtually blind. If you move slowly and stay on the right side of the wind, you can get real close. Pit-barbecued javelina is one of God's gifts to the human tastebud. They love to eat prickly pear. When a javelina bites into a prickly pear pad, s/he typically leaves ragged strands behind. When a rodent eats a pad, the result is usually a very clean semicircle.

Raccoons

Intelligent, inquisitive, courageous and capable of staging vicious attacks on humans, dogs and other irritating creatures. Don't feed them. You only end up creating a wild animal that does not fear you or respect you. They, like all wild animals, have a place in the world. That place is wild and out in nature. Coons are predominantly predators.

Skunks

Six different types of skunks are found throughout Arizona. If you come across a skunk and he starts to stamp his front feet, you'd best leave. His next step is to try to spray you. The spotted skunk and hooded skunk are particularly beautiful.

gracilis

leucoparia

Spotted skunk. (Reprinted from *Mammals of Arizona* by Donald Hoffmeister, The University of Arizona Press, ©1986. Courtesy The U of A Press.)

Bats

Wonderful predators of the night sky, slaughtering multitudes of insects nightly. A huge variety of bats live in or migrate through Arizona. Not all bats eat insects; some bats eat nectar.

Coyotes

Bright, adjustable. Busy expanding their territory in response to everything thrown against them. This species needs no protection from man. It has proven time and time again that man is no serious match for it. A coyote will eat anything it can, plant or animal. In urban areas they will prey on cats and small dogs.

Cactus Mouse. An inhabitant of desert regions, the cactus mouse feeds on seeds and succulent vegetation. Artwork by Randy Babb.

Desert Shrew. Weighing only about as much as a penny the desert shrew is a ferocious predator. Lizards, invertebrates and other small mammals are all on its menu. Artwork by Randy Babb.

Mountain Lion, Cougar

They do exist along the remote portions of the Verde. You are not likely to see one, even if one is quite close. The only one I have ever seen in the wild was a tawny flash down some rocks along the Salt River. Their tracks are common along the Verde below Childs. I strongly urge you to read *Soul Among Lions* by Harley Shaw. It is thought-provoking and excellent. Cougars require a lot of open territory. They, too, have survived man's best attempts to kill them off. As long as they have sufficient wilderness, the species will do ok.

Big Horn Desert Sheep

Re-established by AGFD with invaluable assistance from the Desert Big Horn Sheep Society. This group of dedicated hunters is THE reason why sheep exist in Arizona at all. Unfortunately, the population re-established along the Verde didn't take well. If you see any, they are remnants of this restocking attempt. AGFD does not believe enough of them have survived to be considered a viable population.

Bobcats, Ringtailed Cats

They hunt all along the Verde. You will undoubtedly be near one if you go into the remote areas at all. You are unlikely to see one, however. Bobcats are feline; ringtails are not. Ringtails are related to raccoons and Procynids.

Muskrats

Most of the rats I have seen have been above Perkinsville.

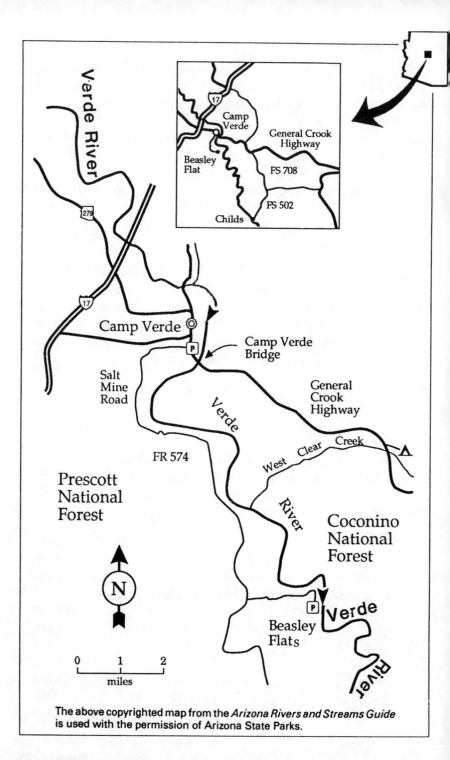

The above copyrighted map from the *Arizona Rivers and Streams Guide* is used with the permission of Arizona State Parks.

Camp Verde to Beasley Flats

Mileage: 10 miles

Elevation Change: 3080 to 2980

Warnings:
- Private land.
- Ugly, dangerous diversion dams.
- Undercut river bank, river left, just below confluence with West Clear Creek.
- Eagle Closures.

Motorized access:
- Bridge where Middle Verde—Camp Verde road (FR 646) crosses the Verde River.
- Salt Mine Road into Beasley Flats (FR 574 to 527 to 334).
- Bridge where General Crook Trail crosses the Verde River. River left, down river side. .
- West Clear Creek, off FR 574.

Days needed: One to two

This is a trip I like in all seasons.

It is always fun to see the awakening of the trees in the spring. In the summer, the green leaves provide visual relief to desert eyes overloaded with brown. The golden leaves reflecting off the water in the fall are incredible. You share the creek with the fallen leaves, as if they were colorful little boats joining you in an armada. Winter allows more expansive views of the Black Hills and Squaw Peak, plus the freedom to appreciate the dark and light interplay of the trunks and branches of the trees.

Immediately after putting on, you will paddle past the mouth of Beaver Creek on river left. Then there are limestone cliffs river left, and benches with big cottonwoods river right. It is pretty and peaceful. Soon you enter a big pool, created by one of the more evil-looking diversion dams on the river. The pool itself is quiet, lined with homes, big trees and the only boat docks I've seen on the Verde. It is possible to rent boat rides here.

> The diversion dam is made from broken cement and rebar. **The rebar stands up from the dam** like so many snakes off the head of Medusa, waiting to strike out at some careless boat or, worse yet, swimmer. At normal flows it is not difficult to safely line or walk your boat through here. At high flows, it is a crap shoot. A friend of mine in a raft once received a four-foot rip in his boat by trying to run this in high water.

Below the dam the creek braids and comes together through a series of marshy ruins and small islands. It is peaceful and intimate. Nothing you encounter is higher than a Class 1. There is almost always enough water for you to stay inside your boat.

This section is rightly attracting attention from anglers (bass and catfish), bird watchers and recreationists who want a different, pleasant day's outing. Some of the local canoe rental companies may rent you a paddler to paddle your canoe, if you want to concentrate on fishing or looking for birds. Other outfitters will rent you an inflatable kayak and provide you lunch. This trip can be divided into half, if you make arrangements with one of the canoe rental places. They can usually get an access point on private land partway into the trip.

There is public land in spots along the trip where you can camp. There are also some private parcels where camping is tolerated if done respectfully. Contact local canoe rental places for details. Their information is most likely to be up to date.

As the trip unfolds, you move closer to the Black Hills. You will also paddle past some very well-to-do homes.

Shortly below the dam, you paddle under the Camp Verde-Strawberry Road. It is also called the General Crook Trail, after an Indian fighter. A river access point and city park is planned for this site.

Gen. Crook operated under the direction of General Sheridan, who operated under General Sherman. During the Civil War, Grant, Sherman and Sheridan reintroduced the concept of winning war by waging total war on the people, not just the armies.

On Grant's orders, Sheridan devastated the Shenandoah Valley. (Grant is reputed to have ordered such destruction that a crow flying down the Valley would have to carry his own rations.) Sherman showed his understanding of this concept on his march through Georgia and then up the coast through the Carolinas. After the war, Sherman and Sheridan came out west and applied these principles to the remaining fighting tribes of Native Americans.

The General Crook Highway is shown on the *Recreation Opportunity Guide: Verde River* map as being located at FRM 69. From here to Sheeps Crossing, at FRM 10, I will present you with two different sets of mile notices: FRM, referring to the *Recreation Opportunity Guide: Verde River* map, and TRM referring to the continuous trip down the Verde from Morgan Ranch.

This entire segment is a restful, pretty and easy paddle down a rural creek. **It is an excellent choice for novice paddlers** or paddlers with children. It is easily reached from Phoenix, Tucson or Flagstaff by traveling I-17. It is possible to rent canoes and shuttle service in Camp Verde, as well as to make arrangements with outfitters in Flagstaff. The scenery and fishing are both noteworthy. This segment is the one I recommend for your first boat trip on the Verde. It is becoming very popular.

The re-entry of a drainage ditch, river left a little less than six miles into the trip, is well worth exploring. There are springs in here, so there is water always, even when the ditch itself is dry.

Below West Clear Creek the river pushes against some high white cliffs and turns right. These cliffs are undercut. That means a swimmer who gets swept up against them could find himself underneath them. The undercut is not very deep, but it would be important for a person who was swept underneath not to panic, but to calmly push off the cliffs to escape.

You are likely to miss the mouth of West Clear Creek at TRM 84, since what water that does flow usually enters without fanfare. From the Verde, the mouth often appears to be just an extensive rock bar on river left. This is another spot where the Forest Service plans to add river bank campgrounds. You move past more cottonwoods and gain sights of Squaw Peak, which is the geographic center of Arizona. The river curves east, then northeast to find a way around Beasley Flats. Hitting another set of cliffs river left, the creek turns south. (The quick water at thse cliffs is called "Rollo Uno" or "Numero Uno" by some paddlers.)

You are now paddling along Beasley Flats. There are a number of possible takeouts. Most folk go to the Forest Service river access point, where you can drive right down to the creek. This site has been turned into a developed site, using SLIF monies.

You, and the Verde, are at FRM 59.5 when you reach this access point, about 88 and one-half miles below Morgan Ranch.

Smiles reward travelers who plan trips
within the limits of children.

Young paddler demonstrates kneeling technique
when paddling a rapid.

Reptiles and Amphibians

Lizards

Geckos

These yellow critters grow up to five inches long. Yellow-skinned with brown bands. They are largely nocturnal. The only times I have seen them is when I turn over piles of trash or debris. Geckos feed on insects and spiders.

Zebra-tailed Lizards

Fast, reaching speeds of 15 miles per hour. As the name indicates, the tail is striped (underneath, especially). The rest of the lizard is grayish. They grow to eight inches long. Feed on insects and spiders.

Gila Monster

Legally protected. Poisonous. You are very unlikely to see it. Eats eggs, rodents and lizards.

Tiger Salamander. The tiger salamander spends most of its life secreted in subterranean burrows, coming to the surface only during the rainy seasons and in the spring to breed. Artwork by Randy Babb.

Greater-eared, Lesser-eared

The difference is the overall size of the animal, not the ears. Both are grey-brown with Greater somewhat darker than the Lesser. The Greater can reach nine inches, the Lesser five inches. Both prey on insects and spiders.

Collared

Identified by a black and white neck band. Eats insects and small reptiles. Can get to 10 inches and they do bite.

Side blotched (Spiny)

Has blue black blotches behind the forelegs. Usually under five inches. Likes to munch on insects, scorpions and ticks.

Regal Horned, Short Horned

The famous horned "toads," which are actually lizards. The Short Horned is the more widespread. Both versions chow on ants. The short horned bear live young.

Short Horned Lizard. Artwork by Randy Babb.

Whiptails

Up to 10 inches long. Very quick animals. Stripes run along the body. Some of the subdivisions, such as Chihuahua's, seem to be made up of all females, reproducing without fertilization.

Non-Poisonous Snakes

Common Kingsnakes

Brightly-banded with black and yellow, these get to five feet long. They are constrictors. They kill their prey by squeezing it so tightly that the prey cannot take a breath and dies from suffocation.

Gopher (Bullsnakes)

Big and heavy-bodied constrictors, reaching six feet in length. Active chasing rodents in the daytime. Is often mistaken for a rattler, as it will, when threatened, flatten its head, hiss and vibrate its tail. If that tail is in dry leaves, a rattling sound is produced.

Garters

Long, horizontal stripes. Under three feet long. Swims well and likes the water, pursuing frogs, tadpoles, fish and salamanders. All garter snakes (there are several types) release a foul-smelling musk and **bite aggressively** when handled.

Poisonous Snakes

You are not likely to see a poisonous snake. They are out there. They just don't want to meet you, so they don't call themselves to your attention. If you do see a poisonous snake, it will probably be a rattler. If you see it along the Verde or its tributaries, it will probably be a western diamondback.

Western Diamondback

Can be a **BIG** snake, up to seven feet long. Preys upon rodents, small mammals, lizards and birds. All rattlers possess heat-sensing abilities which allow them to strike with undiminished accuracy in total darkness at warm-blooded prey.

Coral Snakes

There are no records of fatalities in Arizona due to the bite of this small, shy snake. Unlike the rattler, which injects its poison, corral snakes must chew their venom into a wound. Largely nocturnal, always under 15 inches in length, they feed on lizards and snakes.

Turtles and Tortoises

Desert Tortoise

Land animal. You are not likely to see one. Leave it alone if you do. They have enough problems without dealing with your intrusive behavior.

Desert Tortoise. Artwork by Randy Babb.

Sonora Mud Turtle

The most commonly-encountered turtle along the Verde. Five inches long and colored grey/olive. Feeds on aquatic insects.

Soft-Shelled Turtle

An exotic rarely found along the Verde. Good. The introduction of exotics usually means trouble for the native population. If you happen to catch one (they have soft shells and are hard to misidentify), do the native populations a favor. Eat it.

Amphibians

Woodhouse Toad

Three-to-four inches long. Colored brown/grey with a pale stripe down its back. Its call resembles the bawl of a calf.

Great Plains Toad

Three to four inches. Green mottled with brown. Has a call like an air-hammer.

Red Spotted Toad

I see lots of these, one to two inches long. Grey body with red warts. Call is a long trill.

Leopard Frog

Green with spots. Four to five inches long. Look for them near marshy areas that have cattails.

Canyon Tree Frog

Grey/brown with dark spots. Two inches long. Their call is a trill.

Bullfrog

An eight-inch exotic. Good to eat.

"Off-the-Wall" rapids provide challenge
as low as 50 cfs (Camp Verde).

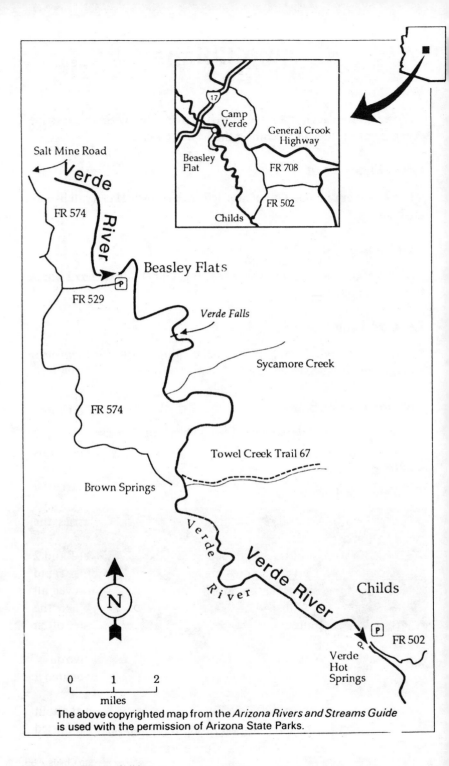

The above copyrighted map from the *Arizona Rivers and Streams Guide* is used with the permission of Arizona State Parks.

Beasley Flats to Childs

Mileage: 18 miles

Elevation Change: 2980 to 2695

Warnings: ● Multiple rapids
      ● Two falls
      ● Fences
      ● Eagle closures
      ● Some private property

Motorized access:
- Beasley Flats, using Salt Mine Road (FR 574 to 529 to 332).
- Childs, using FR 708 and 502.
- Gap Creek, using FR 574. **It is not legal to drive to the river at this point.** The walk to the river is less than half-a-mile.

Trails: Trail 67 out of the Childs area follows part of the river along the ridge on river left.

Days needed: One at high flows. Two at low flows. Take more if you can. There is much to explore.

This is known as the whitewater section of the Verde. It contains both the greatest concentrations of notable rapids and the highest-classed rapids on the entire Verde. It is one of the sections of Arizona rivers which has been noted as special by the U.S. Congress. It is part of the Federal Wild and Scenic Rivers system and it carries the classification of "Scenic."

If we look at most of the rapids themselves, they are level 1 and 2 only. (Remember, Class 3 requires maneuvering in current. **A rapid can be big and uncomfortable and still be only a Class 2.**) However, all of these rapids occur in isolated, very rough country. When the whitewater is most intense, the water and air temperature are often cold.

I've boated this section at 47 cfs (Camp Verde) and it took two days. I was out of my boat a good bit, dragging over rock bars. I've boated it at 2000 cfs (Camp Verde) and the trip has taken four hours.

Novice canoeists will notice the rapids gaining some push at about 200 cfs. At 500 cfs, the river has a lot of push but has not yet buried many of the rocks. This is the level when the very first larger rowing rafts may appear. It is my favorite level. I love the technical demands of dodging all those rocks. Since the river doesn't flow at this level regularly, no clear channel is created. It is a fast run through irregular obstacles.

By the time the river has risen to 800 cfs some of the requirements to be a technically-skilled boater are dropped as the water buries the rocks. However, hydraulics begin to form, both standing waves and holes, so a different type of advanced boating skill is needed. As the river rises past 800 cfs, rafters and kayakers start to increase the population of boaters. From 1500 cfs up, the hydraulics can be very large and powerful. At 2000 cfs, holes exist that can turn a badly paddled 16-foot canoe into a wildly flipping visual spectacular. I know this from experience.

Below Beasley Flats, the river starts calm. In an easy sort of way it quickly runs south up against some cliffs, then turns away to the east. When it hits its next sharp turn (south, then southeast), there is the first rapid of note.

Called "Rollo Tres" or "Numero Tres" by many local boaters and "Off the Wall" by the Forest Service, **this drop has disconcerted many a novice boater.**

Immediately above "Off the Wall" on river left is an area known as Cottonwood Basin. At this pool I had one of the more wonderful experiences of my life.

While on my headwater to confluence Verde canoe trip, I left Beasley Flats at 6:30 in the morning. I dropped into the pool just above "Off The Wall" rapid at about 7 a.m.

An underwater disturbance along the reeds caught my attention. Again, it was an otter who had just caught a fish. A full-grown otter, this time, two feet or more long.

The otter resurfaced and began eating breakfast. The eddy currents drifted me closer to the animal. The crunching as the otter chewed through the bones seemed loud enough to echo off the nearby cliffs.

I drifted too close. The otter dove and reappeared a few yards further away, half-eaten fish dangling from its mouth. Again, I pushed my welcome. The mammal dove and reappeared without the fish, but in the company of another full grown otter. We played tag all over that pool. I would try to creep close enough for a camera shot. The otters are curious animals and they clearly wanted to know what in the hell I was. They would raise nine inches or so of their body out of the water and bob their heads side to side, trying to get a better view.

Once they both climbed up on a rock, as if to confer, while peering intently at me. Finally, they dove underwater and swam off down the rapid. Well, I was going that direction, too. At the bottom of the rapid, one otter broke surface as I paddled past, standing quietly as the current pushed me downstream, restoring their privacy.

"Off The Wall" is located about 1.5 miles below Beasley Flats. It is created by the outflow of a drainage that enters river left. The river is forced by the deposited material up against the right bank. The water then slides down between the sheer rock wall on the right and the rock bar on the left. **The drop is hidden behind a bend in the right rock wall.**

At flows above 500 cfs or so it would be possible for an inattentive boater to be swept into this drop. Especially if they were paddling along the river right.

The rapid is something like 30 yards long, with a little bit of remnants beyond that. It contains pillow rocks, holes and laterals. At lower flows it can be a very uncomfortable swim.

It seems visually intimidating to many novice boaters, but it is only a Class 2. No real maneuvering is required. A boater who only floated through would make it something over 50 percent of the time. Because of the **number of rocks close to the surface** of the water it is an unpleasant rapid for a wrong-side up kayaker.

I paddled this section once with two kayakers, one of whom was new to the sport, at about 400 cfs. This guy had successfully paddled the "day stretch" of the Salt, which is considered to be more difficult than this section of the Verde.

He flipped over at the top of this rapid, abandoned his boat and swam the rapid, but not before learning why the slang name for a helmet is "brain bucket." He lost his confidence. He walked virtually every rapid after that, almost all of which were easier than stuff he had paddled successfully on the Salt.

As the bend unwinds, low levels can show rocks with some pushy, uncooperative currents.

PAY ATTENTION!

As you approach your next bend (to the southeast), you will (damn sight better) notice islands in the middle of the creek and a drainage entering river right. You are a little over two miles below Beasley Flats.

Just paddle for shore (I suggest river left above the islands)to do some scouting. You are going to have to decide how you are going to deal with the Prefalls and Falls of the Verde.

The Falls is downstream of the island. The Prefalls is in the left channel around the island. If you scout from the right bank, you will not see the Prefalls. If you run the right channel, you will not run the Prefalls, but you may as well look at it.

Both drops involve sheer drops. Prefalls drops three feet or so. The Falls is closer to six. High water will fill in both drops. By the time you have 2000 cfs there is no vertical drop of water, though there is noticeable turbulence, holes and laterals.

The risks involved in running these drops vary with the water levels. I have paddled both and walked both. I have paddled the Prefalls and walked the Falls. I have gone river right to avoid the Prefalls and then paddled the Falls.

Don't get swept into these drops by accident! It is possible. It is especially possible to get swept into the Prefalls by accident.

Running the Falls at higher levels has certain risks also. Immediately below the Falls is a long, narrow mini canyon which I like to call Foul Rift.

> At high flows this gorge, cut through the basalt, runs swift with current and is dotted with rapids. Eddies are minimal and minimalistic. It is possible (I know from experience) to lose it at the Falls and be swept down river half-a-mile before being able to self-rescue.

Nesting eagles downstream come with their own eagle watchers. These folk keep an eye on the birds and also on fool or idiot boaters who disturb the nest. You may find that such a swim and subsequent rescue get written up in a government document, and may be used as evidence for the need to close the Verde to paddlers during the nesting season.

Don't run the Falls unless you know that you can be rescued quickly downstream, in the event you miscalculate.

Those who run the Falls tend to do it either extreme river right or extreme river left, depending on the type of thrills they prefer. Those who like to drop off a sheer drop will run extreme river left. Extreme river right gets most of the flow and has eroded more.

There are a couple of rocks immediately downstream that create holes. I like to run river right. I still get the challenge of trying to hit the exact right spot. I don't get to run a sheer drop, but the right side is steep. Finally, the nature of the right side is that running it tends to feed you right into one or more of the holes below. I like to play in the holes.

I don't run the Falls at low water. I do run the Prefalls at low water. I don't run the Prefalls at high water, unless adequate safety procedures can be established. It's not that the Prefalls is that dangerous. It is the presence of the Falls immediately down stream. I typically run the Falls at any level above 350 cfs (Camp Verde) or so. I do know boaters who have run this section of the Verde at levels of 10,000 to 40,000 cfs (Camp Verde). They talk of sharing the river with **uprooted trees, long expanses of ripped-out barbed wire fences, and a house trailer or two.**

Once you exit Foul Rift (the sadly unnamed but beautiful basalt canyon) El Rio Verde slows down until you get to Chasm Creek (river right). At lower levels, there is one bouncy rapid decorated with a hole and tree about half-a-mile below Chasm.

You can recognize the Chasm Creek area by looking for the river crossing cart cable for the USGS flow gauge located here. This cart is put in so that workers can hike in and get to the gauge from either side of the river, regardless of water level, should the gauge need servicing.

Chasm Creek is worth noting for another reason. Starting just below Chasm, you encounter a mile-long stretch of quick water with four distinct drops at lower water. At high water it all merges into one, mildly (by whitewater standards) turbulent push. This section is the most challenge (fun) at levels near 500 cfs (Camp Verde).

Rock bars are typically created by the outflow of some drainage, in this case, the Chasm Creek and Sycamore Creek drain gauges. These rocks are deposited by floods and rearranged by floods. It stands to reason, then, that channels will be ill-defined and changeable from flood to flood.

As you run these dops, you will notice a series of larger boulders near the center-right. Your least-obstructed route (and the one with the most push) is most often found near these boulders.

Sycamore Creek enters this one-mile section of drop about halfway down on the river left. It enters a downstream angle, and you are often otherwise occupied when you pass it. It is not uncommon for paddlers to paddle the Verde numerous times and not notice its entry.

This series of rapids ends as the river piles up against a river cliff and makes a very short turn to the north. It then is thwarted again by cliffs in its futile attempt to avoid its downstream fate and goes toward the east.

The next couple of miles move swiftly, with only a couple of rock bars to provide paddling entertainment. About seven miles below Beasley (FRM 52.75), the river turns to the southeast. As the river straightens, there exists at low water a small (two-foot) waterfall set at a diagonal from river right going up to the left.

There is an eroded channel at the top of the diagonal. No matter. It's usually easier just to run the falls. This gets buried pretty quickly as the water level increases.

PAY ATTENTION! The river will hit a cliff wall and turn south. At FRM 52 there is a notable rapid, called Punk Rock by everyone except the Forest Service. The Forest Service calls it Turkey Gobbler Rapid.

Punk Rock Rapid runs down against a cliff, **forcing a sudden, sharp turn to the river left.** Large boulders have fallen off the cliff at the apex of the turn, sharpening and lengthening it. The current has fought back at this arrogant intrusion by forcing a couple of very small channels through the boulders. The rocks do succeed in diverting almost all the water to the left around the last and largest boulder, which is Punk Rock.

At higher levels the current simply buries the whole shebang, including Punk Rock. At these levels a large, intimidating but not unfriendly hole develops downstream of Punk Rock.

I have fun in this rapid at every level above 40 cfs and below 2000 cfs (Camp Verde). It can be a good rapid for novice whitewater boaters to try at higher levels, as there is a substantial pool immediately below, allowing for quick rescue or recovery.

There are sandy beaches on both sides of the river below the rapid which make for good picnic, camping or resting spots.

> At low levels (below 80 cfs at Camp Verde), there is an acknowledgeable risk of a midstream pin upstream of Punk Rock. If you find yourself too far to the right, there is also a **risk of being pinned into one of the small channels** to the right of Punk Rock. **At all levels, the current will want to carry you right smack dab into** (or over) **Punk Rock.** If the current is not flowing over the Rock, it will pillow up against it, giving you a last minute advantage to get around.

If the current is flowing over the rock, only your paddling skill will keep you from going into the large, intimidating, but reasonably friendly hole. (A hole is "friendly" if it allows a paddler, or swimmer, to escape with a minimum of resistance. It is also considered "friendly" if it has a minimum of smaller rocks buried within it. These smaller rocks are one of the many reasons why whitewater boaters wear helmets.) Punk Rock can be scouted from either side. I usually have folk scout it from river left.

Below Punk Rock, the Verde dodges some big rocks and flows over a few small rock bars. You pass the entrance of Towel Creek river left and Gap Creek river right. About one-mile below Punk Rock the river pools up against a river right cliff and a very large rock bar that blocks the entire main channel. You have arrived at Bushman Rapid.

Bushman was named for a tree that was inconveniently placed in the only boatable channel. Eventually, some river runner went into Bushman at very low levels and sawed the offender off. The drop still has plenty of challenge and fun. The stump has new growth and may soon again eat boaters.

The channel is to the extreme river left. It takes off to the left, traveling only a very short distance before it hits a very steep bank and is forced to turn to the right. The top of the drop can be too shallow to boat at levels much below 150 cfs.

Once over the initial shallow area, canoes can traverse the rest at almost all levels. The drop down to the steep bank is **steep**, with some inconveniently-placed rocks. If you successfully make the turn (the current pillowed on the bank will assist you), you will find yourself in a narrow chute, with pushy current, rocks and holes.

At higher flows (above 1000 cfs at Camp Verde), the standing waves at the base of this chute can reach five foot peak to trough. You are paddling past a rock bar, so at high flows some of the water will also be flowing over the rock bar at a right angle to you, creating lateral currents and waves.

Immediately below the rapid is a water gap. Usually this fence is but a single strand. It is not difficult to get under, but it can be **difficult to see**. Just below the fence, on river right, the outflow from Brown Spring can be found.

If you have made it this far and have been comfortable with your experience, the next couple of miles will seem easy. There are some drops, some chances of pins. Nothing real threatening (unless you can't unpin your boat). The only named rapid is one that shows as Rocky Split on the Forest river runners map. I have seen a lot of javelina in this section, usually on the right bank.

At FRM 49 you will pass Gospel Hollow on the left. Looking downstream, you will see some white cliffs extending out from the left bank. They announce White Flash, which is the last rapid most riverrunners consider significant enough to name. This is a pretty straightforward affair. At higher levels, the current will flow over the rocky ledges extending out from the left bank and create some holes.

A lot of paddlers get swept into these holes, even though they are not difficult to avoid. No real matter. There is a pool immediately below which allows for rescue or recovery.

The rest of the ride to Childs (six more miles) have rock bars, pools, rock gardens, chutes, and laterals, but nothing more difficult than you have already seen.

The scenery offers some very pleasant views, especially of the Towel Peaks off the to the left between FRMs 45-48. Pay attention to the left and you will see a small rocky cliff with a lot of barrel cactus, one of the highest latitude concentrations I have noticed in my trips down the Verde. You are starting to enter a new biotic zone.

About one mile above the Childs campground (the campground below Childs referred to as RAP on the Forest Service river runner guide), you encounter an island. Most of the flow goes to the left. The various signs painted on the river right rocks announce that the hot springs is on the right bank, and that you should expect nudity (among other things).

If you want to go the springs (worth a visit) take the right channel. At 100 cfs and above, canoeists can get through most of it. Below that it gets pretty shallow and you will be out dragging your boat. You can't miss the springs.

In the 1920s a resort was built there, but it burned down in the 1950s and rebuilding was not permitted (this is US Forest land). Situated at the end of the "whitewater" run of the Verde, it provides a welcome, warm rush after a day of paddling winter snow melt.

It is a beautiful spot. There is a pool outside where you can soak and look at the mountains and a surviving palm tree. There is a shallow pool inside where you can look at graffiti painted on the walls (some beautiful and creative, some low class and obscene).

This spot offers other things, too. You can run into all sorts of strange, weird people. Some are just fried granolas left over from the 60s, but others are a little bit peculiar. It used to be possible to drive up to a campground virtually across from the hot springs, going through the little village of Childs. This ended after years when the Childs folk had to deal with careless gun play at the camp ground, ORV jerks driving around their homes, rude fools, rude drunken fools driving at excessive speeds past their children at play and perverts who attempted to lure their small daughters into "games."

Most of the folk found here are harmless. A substantial percentage are pretty inconsiderate with regards to trash and the level at which they play their music. Some are sick and offensive.

> You should also know that it is possible to get some pretty serious diseases from hot springs. This can be avoided somewhat by restricting your use to those times when a lot of water is flowing and the exchange rate within the pools is higher.

Don't wash in the springs themselves. Take a bucket and use the warm water to rinse the soap from you in a location where the soap does not enter the springs.

There is a lot of nudity at this hot springs, along with the open use of alcohol and drugs. Still, it is a beautiful spot. If substantial folk of integrity don't go here, then it will end up the territory of worthless leeches.

There is an official camping area here along with one of the foulest toilets known to mankind. The toilets are bad enough that many folk use spots far from their camp (and close to yours). You can pick these spots out. They mark them with toilet paper. In spite of that, it is a beautiful spot for camping. However, the heavy use often results in no available firewood, so bring your own.

The campground is downstream from the end of the island on the left, immediately below the power plant and release of Fossil Springs. You, and the Verde, are at FRM 42.5 and TRM 106.

A hard draw stroke helps avoid collision with Punk Rock.

Punk Rock Rapid at 90 cfs (Camp Verde)
Photo by Wayne House

Arthropods

Damsel Fly. Photo by Steven J. Prchal. Courtesy Sonoran Arthropod Studies, Inc.

Dragonflies (Skimmers and Darners) and Damselflies

Flying predators, searching relentlessly for other flying insects, especially mosquitoes. When dragonflies are at rest, they typically hold their wings to the horizontal. While at rest, Damselflies tend to hold their wings to the vertical. The ones you see flying around joined together, often dipping to the water, are usually Common Skimmers.

Waterboatmen and Backswimmers

You've seen these little black critters. Water boatmen swim rightside up and move around in apparent random fashion. They eat smaller animals and don't bite.

Backswimmers typically swim with their heads down and appear to move more purposefully. They munch on insects, tadpoles, small fish and your fingers.

Water Striders

Everyone likes these bugs. They stay afloat by means of trapped air bubbles in the hairs of their legs. They are predators specializing in small aquatic insects. In the winter they burrow into mud and under rocks.

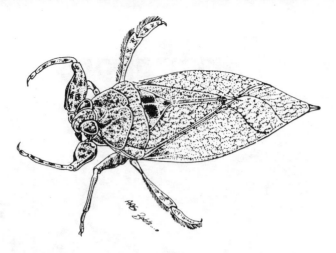

(Courtesy Arizona Game and Fish Department. Artist: Randy Babb)

Giant Water Bugs

I've seen them in all sizes, but they get to be up to two inches long. Their common nickname is "toe bitter." They are aggressive predators that chase down insects, frogs and fish. They inject a mild poison (to you) when they bite.

Fireflies/Lightning Bugs/Glowworms

All of these are some form of beetle, including the glowworms. We don't have large populations in Arizona, but they are out there. I've had my most special sightings along the Verde, and those have been of glowworms. There are many species of lightning bug. Glowworms are either the females or the larvae, depending on the species. All of the species have their own schedule as to when they come out and glow. My sightings of glowworms have been in October on the Wild and Scenic stretch of the Verde. I've also seen isolated glowworms from Camp Verde to Childs in the spring.

Tabanids

A collection of biting flies that include horseflies, deerflies and green heads. It's the females that feed on blood. The larvae are aquatic and are predators.

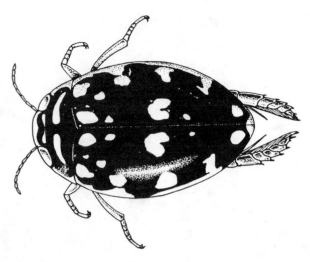

Predaceous Diving Beetle, (Courtesy Arizona Game and Fish Department. Artist: Randy Babb)

Water Beetles

Whirligig beetles swarm on or near the surface looking for prey. They feed on aquatic insects and terrestrial insects that have fallen into the water.

Predaceous Diving Beetles live underwater and are not commonly seen, except by anglers who are netting for hellgrammites.

Crayfish. Photo by Steven J. Prchal. Courtesy Sonoran Arthropod Studies, Inc.

Crayfish

These crustaceans are called crayfish, crawdads or mudbugs. They are found throughout the Verde. Lots of animals, including man, find them delicious. You need a fishing license to capture them. They are excellent fish bait.

Dobson Fly. Photo by Steven J. Prchal. Courtesy Sonoran Arthropod Studies, Inc.

Hellgrammites and Dobson Flies

Turn over rocks in a muddy area, or stir up rocks in the riffles and you are likely to see these common, multi-legged larvae with pincers for jaws. These creatures are the larvae of the Dobsonfly. Hellgrammites are very aggressive predators and they can nip.

Put 10 hellgrammites into a bait can and within 20 minutes at least seven will be all locked into one ball of lethal combat. They are great bait, especially for smallmouth bass. It is best if you clip the small hooks off their back end. Otherwise they lock themselves under rocks and help break your line. I respect these ugly little animals. They just plain don't give up. The parents are bizarre cross-jawed critters. However, they cannot deliver much of a bite.

Scorpions

Twenty to 30 species live in the U.S. The most poisonous threaten only the young or adults in ill health.

Spiders and Relatives

Lots of different species. Harvestmen (Daddy longlegs) prey on insects, suck plant juices and feed on dead animals.

There are 30,000 to 120,000 species of spiders. I can't even begin to describe them. If you boat, you will get lots of them in your boat as you brush underneath overhanging trees and shrubbery. They won't hurt you. One time I knew I was doing a real laid-back trip when I looked down and saw one of my passenger spiders was spinning a web between my knee and the thwart of the canoe.

Some spiders capture their prey with webs (trappers, I guess). Others, like wolf spiders and jumping spiders, hunt their prey and chase it down. Categories of spiders you may see along the Verde include: hairy mygalomorphs (tarantulas), cobweb weavers, sheetweb weavers, orb weavers, nursery web, wolf, and jumping spiders. Spiders are prey for birds, wasps, other spiders and lizards. Spider silk is one of the strongest of natural fibers.

Spider. Photo by Steven J. Prchal. Courtesy Sonoran Arthropod Studies, Inc.

Backyard Bugwatching

Arthropods are the best, yet least utilized, way to introduce a person to wildlife. Watching arthropods does not require binoculars, spotting scopes, blinds or long hours of sitting still. You can find them in your home, yard and under the street lights.

Located in Tucson is an organization dedicated to promoting increased knowledge of arthropods. Sonoran Arthropod Studies, Inc. (SASI) publishes a magazine (*Backyard Bugwatching*), puts on workshops for adults and children, and does research.

I have learned much from these folks. In 1989 they helped 10,000 people learn about bugs, in spite of having a paid staff of less than one. To find out more, write: SASI, P.O. Box 5624, Tucson, AZ 85703, or call 1-602-883-3945.

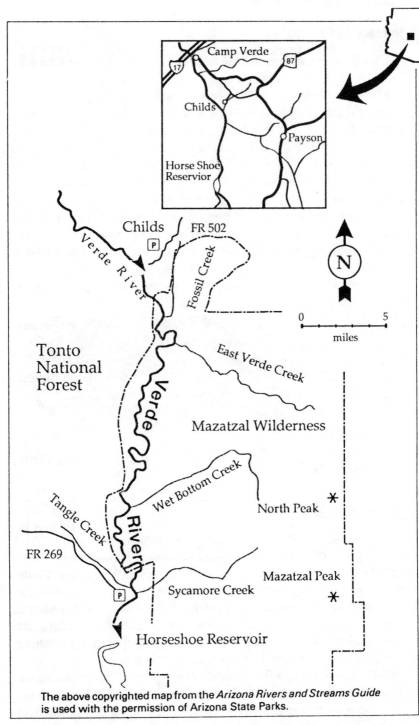

The above copyrighted map from the *Arizona Rivers and Streams Guide* is used with the permission of Arizona State Parks.

Childs to Horseshoe Dam

Childs to Horseshoe Dam

Mileage: 40 miles

Elevation Change: 2695 to 2000

Warnings: ● Nesting eagles
            ● Mud/sand flats at upper end of lake
            ● Potential weird behavior at hot springs

Motorized access:
- Childs - Take FR 708 off the General Crook Highway, then take FR 502 to Childs.
- Red Creek (Four Wheel Drive only) Take FR 269 to FR 18. Not passable if Red Creek is flowing.
- Sheep Bridge—Use FR 269.
- Horseshoe Dam—Use FR 205.

Trails: All of the following trails are shown on the Tonto Forest Map. They are not always maintained. The trails that touch or come very near the river are 11, 41, 17, 20, 22 and 223. It is possible to hike between Childs and Sheep Crossing by using 11 and 41, or 11, 20 and 41.

Days needed: Three to forever.

This section is the most user friendly of all the sections for novice boaters who want to try a little whitewater or who want to boat a little thicker water than what may be available upstream.

> However, the area is remote, remote, remote. This section of river carries the federal designation of "Wild and Scenic" and cuts a Wilderness area. Help, if needed, is a long way away.

The entire trip is beneath rugged desert mountains, as the Verde cuts its way through the Central Highlands. For the first third of the trip, the mountains rise quite quickly from the water. During the latter two thirds of the trip, the river is incising a new, deeper path for itself through its own ancient bed. Down here, the mountains give the river more breathing space.

Childs campground is at FRM 42.5. Immediately after putting on the water you will paddle in a small, lengthy, Class 2 rapid with rocks, holes and waves. The first time the AGFD (Native Fish Program) came through here, they swamped three of three boats (in December). Since then I've been promoting the name "Game and Fish Rapid."

Very quickly, you pass under a major power line, which also serves as the boundary for the Wilderness area. A couple of level 2 rapids come mighty quick, but then the river turns into pools separated by easy drops the whole way to Fossil Creek, 1.5 miles down river.

Below Fossil Creek is a notable rapid, Nasty Little Dogleg. It is a rock bar angled across the river. The current drops over the bar into a narrow slot between the rock bar and the rocky bank. This narrow slot has pushy current, along with a hole and a rock or two. Nasty Little Dogleg is fun and runnable by many novices. However, you would want to choose to run it and not just get swept in. At low water getting swept in is not a threat. At higher water it might be.

The rapid, though not difficult by white water standards, can be visually intimidating to beginners. **Some knowledge on how to control a boat in fast current** and **how to deal with lateral waves** is useful. A swim is not catastrophic as long as the boat is not irretrievably pinned. There is a lengthy pool below, which allows recovery.

> At higher water, this rapid is not for beginners. The narrow slot will turn into a pushy boiling affair.

Some years ago I did an October canoe trip from Childs to Sheep Crossing. I had warm weather, excellent fishing and good rabbit hunting.

The week after I took off, a good friend of mine put on with a small flotilla of canoes, overloaded with gear and children. It had been raining but was forecast to quit. It rained while they put on at Childs. It continued to rain as they paddled the four miles to the mouth of Fossil Creek.

That afternoon the skies opened up with rain and hail as they set up camp above Nasty Little Dogleg rapid. The water level stayed firm and steady, at about 150-200 cfs.

The next morning the view from their tents was quite different. The river was running close to 20,000 cfs. The water through Nasty Little Dogleg was five vertical feet higher than the night before. It took them two days to walk back to Childs, lining their canoes from shore.

Below Fossil Creek a large island shows on the topo maps. This island exists only at higher flows. At normal flows, all the water descends the river right channel. The trip around this "island" is shallow and rocky, with one very deceptive little rapid part way into your descent. **Be on the lookout for a good-sized boulder out in the current.**

At levels below 200 cfs (Camp Verde) the left channel is totally obstructed, but from above the right channel appears boatable.

> It IS boatable, if you manage to avoid the two hidden rocks immediately over the lip of the drop. If you don't avoid them, you have pinned your boat in very fast current at the beginning of a trip through Wilderness.

If I am heavily-loaded, I drag around over the left channel.

This island, and the steady low level rapids, don't end until TRM 111 (FRM 38), at which point the river is going south. At TRM 112, it is going due north. At TRM 113, it is again headed south.

> The scenery throughout is rugged and beautiful. Visually, you are left with no doubt that this is a wilderness river. The hills are high, rugged and close to the river.

At about TRM 113.5, you enter a couple of closely-spaced pools. At the bottom of these pools, at FRM 36 (TRM 113.6), the East Verde squeezes from between Cedar Bench and Limestone Hills to join the Verde and create an excellent fishing spot.

It's a nice spot just to sit and watch the workings of light, vegetation, hill and water. It offers good hiking, either bushwhacking or along the #11 trail which passes just above the juncture of the two Verdes. There is a large sandy area for camping (river left) which is favored by hikers, horsemen and boaters, so firewood is occasionally an issue.

It is a magnificent spot. Wild, remote, the land around you is virtually untouched. The sky does not escape lights from Phoenix, 60 miles away, which create a definite area of light pollution in the downriver sky.

There used to be a large, long island just below the East Verde. It is now a peninsula.

Portions of the old channel remain and alternate dry sections with pools. Much of it is crowded with trees and shrubs. From a fish biologist's point of view, it is a much more interesting habitat than the main channel. My knowledge of and appreciation of the total river has grown considerabley from my association with AGFD fish biologists.

I had such an arrogant riverrunner mentality. I thought I knew rivers. Now, I also appreciate the shallow backwaters that provide important habitat for the smaller fish. Before, I barely even noticed them.

The Verde is headed for its first contact with Squaw Butte. It touches Houston Creek at FRM 34.4 and flows past the base of the Butte. If you have looked up from the creek as you paddled down to this point, you have already caught a glimpse or two of the Butte. You can still see it when you arrive at FRM 14, if you climb up away from the river.

At FRM 32.7 is good camping near the USGS gauge. There are trees, and it is grassy. You may also find critters in the camp. While I have seen quite a few rattlers in Arizona and maybe three coral snakes, I have only seen one rattler and one coral snake along the banks of the Verde or its major tribs. I saw both of them on the same day at this spot. Skunks often inhabit the nearby rocks.

About seven-tenths of a mile below the USGS gauge, you descend Redwall Rapid, then Tree Row Rapid and paddle into a pool with a noticeable spring emerging from the left bank. This spring is thermal. It's not all that warm, only about body temperature. In the past, other folk with beaver in their blood have tried to create a pool in this rocky hillside. They have managed to put together one that reaches your ankles. The thermal impact on the pool below does make for some interesting fishing when the rest of the river is cold.

From here on the river is dominated by pools and low level rapids. The scenery is great, as is the fishing in warmer weather. Below Childs, the only places to legally drive into the river are Red Creek and Sheep Crossing. Many paddlers put in at Childs and take out at Red Creek, or put on at Childs and take out at Sheep Bridge, or put on at Red Creek and take out at Sheep Bridge, or put on at any of the upstream points and take out at Horseshoe Dam.

This entire segment is big, rugged and remote. After more than eight trips through here, I have just started to explore it. I spent some 20 days boating the entire Verde River. I could happily spend 20 days just between Childs and Horseshoe Dam.

One hundred and nineteen miles into the river, at FRM 31, Goat Camp Canyon enters from the left. Pete's Cabin Mesa is just below. Trails #11 and 20 are running up on the top of the inner gorge on the left. Number 11 comes down and crosses the river just above an unnamed drainage that enters river right.

If you're attentive, you will see the telephone pole(!) with the metal hiker sign on it, river left. This is a good spot to camp. If you get up on the trail and walk down river, pay attention to the saguaros to your right. **One of them has a prickly pear growing out of it,** about eight to nine feet in the air.

Look across the river at the high ridges. The North and Middle branches of Red Creek are behind that wall, flowing in the same direction as the Verde they seek to join.

At FRM 28 the river turns east, then south, then west as it works its way around Canoe Mesa. The entire area on river left is cut with a number of very interesting drainages. It is a great area for hiking (bushwhacking or along the trail).

Some of these creeks have perennial water not far from their confluence with the Verde, even if they appear dry at the confluence itself. Surprisingly, most of them have had their native fish populations destroyed by the introduction of exotics. Where did these exotics (sunfish, mostly) come from? Were they washed downstream to this point from stocked waters higher up? Did they swim up here during high water times? Did Bait Bucket Charlie bring them in? Who knows? But here they are.

Just as the river makes its final turn around Canoe Mesa, it is bordered by Mule Shoe, a deep entrenched meander, on the left. At FRM 26, the start of the neck of Mule Shoe, the river is headed west. Three miles later it will be a little over one mile away, after traveling west, north, west, south, southeast, southwest, east and northeast. In this three miles you will paddle Gauntlet Rapid, a number of other small rapids and pass a small, river-level cave.

One hundred twenty-six-and-a-half miles into its trip, the Verde River hits Table Mountain (FRM 23.4). The river will bounce away from that impact and return to hit the mountain one more time. Wet

Bottom Mesa appears on the left at about FRM 22. Behind that mesa, Wet Bottom Creek is traveling southwest between Razorback Mountain and Upper and Lower Racetrack Mesas as it aims for the Verde. Mell of a Hess Rapid is negotiated and then, at FRM 19.75, you are at Red Creek.

> It is possible to drive here, if you have a four-wheel drive, if Red Creek is not flowing, and if the road isn't too muddy. Unfortunately, this means Driving Destroyers can get in here and the place will often show it.*

Red Creek is a lovely spot. At the creek's edge are a number of cottonwoods and other large trees. As you would expect, the outflow from Red Creek does create a rapid. In this case, the rapid is long and shallow. Again, as you would expect, the outflow also creates a pool.

The pool at Red Creek is one of the many Verde gems. Deep, bordered with small cliffs on the right and trees and rocks on the left, it offers swimming and the chance at fish. I talked to a paddler who claimed to have pulled a 20-pound cat from this pool. Perhaps, even if I allow for angler inflation, I'm sure he caught a good-sized fish.

About one mile below Red Creek, Wet Bottom Creek enters from the left, creating Wet As Rapids (this is not a misspelling). Shortly below the entrance of Wet Bottom, the Verde runs smack into a large bedrock.

To the left of the rock is a very large recirculating eddy, often packed with floating diftwood. Unseen by riverrunners, immediately behind that rock, is a deep depression in the bedrock, which usually has some amount of water in it. If you fish it not too long after a flood, you can sometimes catch some hungry cats or bass that have found themselves trapped by falling waters.

Just before the Verde hits the next set of cliffs and turns left, is an alkaline seep river right. **It is not legal to drive into here.**

By the time you have reached FRM 15, 135 miles into the Verde's journey, Tangle Peak is on your right with Cedar Mountain rising behind. High banks and riparian growth may force you to climb the

---

*This spot has been adopted by the Arizona 4 x 4 Explorers and the area has improved under the care of these dedicated volunteers.

left bank to get a good view. It is worth your while to get out and climb a bit, anyway. All of the twists and turns the Verde has been making have been incising down into an ancient flood plain.

It is not necessary to climb too far uphill to be rewarded with some amazing upstream views. Paddlers too often get as locked into their boats as motorists do within their vehicles. Bright spots of green high on Tangle Peak lead me to suspect the presence of springs. They are on my to-be-explored list.

Many of my sightings of glowworms have been on this Wild and Scenic stretch of the Verde. The worms I've seen have been small (quarter-inch, maybe) and had a lighting cycle of about 10 seconds. You have to get away from your fire to see them. When they are active, they crawl up into the wet, muddy, grassy or marshy edges and start signaling. It is as if the river is wearing a cool necklace of soft, small, blinking lights.

I have hunted this area, also, as I have much of the Verde. The quail and waterfowl hunting are best from King Canyon to Cottonwood. Javelina are found from King Canyon to Perkinsville and along the entire river below Beasley Flats. Below Beasley is my favorite for muledeer and calling predators. Transporting your big game out by canoe is preferable to quartering it and backpacking it out any day. Predator callers can hope for lions as well as coyotes in this remote and wonderful section of the Verde.

After you round the bend below FRM 14, you float a long pool. Spend some time fishing for bass under the overhanging branches. When the leaves are changing, this is beautiful. One fall I had so much fun I paddled back up to the top of the pool just to be able to do it again.

As you close in on some high white bluffs and the river turns to the left, you will hit a surprising little rapid on the apex of that turn. At FRM 11, 140 miles from Morgan Ranch, you flow into a large and spectacular pool created by the outflow from Tangle Creek.

Red rocks and cliffs coat both banks. Heavy growths of large reeds add color and movement. Sometimes I just sit here to let the trip this far catch up and soak in. Once the Tangle creek rapids start, they last the whole way to Sycamore Creek (#2).

At FRM 10, you have reached Sheep Bridge, complete with hiker's bridge and hot springs. The bridge, used in the past to run sheep, has been rebuilt to serve backpackers and hikers. The hikes up Sycamore and Horse canyons are worthwhile.

This is a totally unimproved campground. No toilet, but lots of toilet paper. No firewood. Weird behavior. The hot springs are two large tubs hidden in the reeds. I like it. I believe this hot springs has a better water exchange rate than the one at Childs. I am more comfortable using it. I never camp here.

> More decent folk should visit here and pressure Congress to provide the Forest adequate money to tend to this place appropriately.

This is another spot that begs for adoption by a four-wheel drive club. Only increased use and scrutiny by organized ethical users will save this unique area from repeated abuse. Hunters' organizations will periodically organize themselves to watch a certain hunt. They try to make contact with the hunters assigned to that hunt to let them know that there will be extra eyes in the field and to encourage the nimrods to practice their sport ethically. It would be perfect if a four-wheel-drive club would set up a similar watch over this area during a known heavy use time.

A lot of folk choose to leave the river at Sheep Bridge. I do about 80 percent of the time. However, you may want to paddle the remaining eight miles or so to Horseshoe Dam. It is a somewhat easier access point to drive to and you may want to pursue the bass that congregate in the lightly-fished upper end of the lake. Or, you may be looking to hunt the remote right side of upper Horseshoe Lake, especially for javelina.

What you encounter here will very much depend on what is happening to the lake. If the lake is very high, you will hit lake water not far below Sheep Bridge. If it is low, you will hit a mile-long stretch of sand and mud flats about five miles into your trip.

Between TRM 141 and 144, the creek runs along trees and cliffs, past Ister Flat. There is motorized access here on river left. As you drop, notice the lake effect. Driftwood is piled differently, since it is placed by wind and not current.

The bankside growth is different, too. Lakes favor salt cedar and this aggressive exotic begins to choke out our native trees. As you make your final touch on Chalk Mountain, you can see a line of dead cottonwood trunks. They mark the old creek bank, killed by the rising waters of the lake.

Horseshoe Lake varies quite a bit in water level. It is also a shallow lake. These two characteristics help make it a very good fish producer, especially at the upper end. When the lake level drops, plants move in to reclaim the mudflats. When the water rises, these plants drown and rot, releasing a wealth of nutrients into the water. These nutrients are fodder for fish and the creatures fish prey on. If the water level does not drop again, starvation will set in after the plants have finished rotting and the lake, any lake, becomes a lifeless, watery desert.

Dead calm is my favorite condition in which to paddle a lake, day or night. With virtually no effort, you can establish a steady, mile-eating pace. Paddling through the reflections of the mountains or trees is a magic time. On a calm, clear night paddling a lake is like paddling through the sky itself in human-powered space travel.

Lakes are good for seeing far away scenery, also. As you cross Horseshoe, you have a good look at the Mazatzals on your left. To your right is Sunset Mountain, Humboldt Mountain, and Rover Peak. The deep cut you pass on the right just before you get to the takeout by the dam is Lime Creek.

Horseshoe Dam is at FRM 0. It is about 150 miles below where we started down El Rio de Los Reyes.

Fishing a wilderness pool beneath ancient ruins
of surrounding mountains.

Bullrushes and trees create a paradise
for red-winged blackbirds.

Lazy summer canoeing on the Verde.

No-Trace Camping

We are concentrating more and more recreationists into our available space. The impact of too many loving folk on a resource can be disastrous. The problem can be particularly acute along our riparian zones for a number of reasons. Riparian zones are one of the rarest habitats in North America. People seem naturally attracted to water. State Park and Forest Service statistics both show that the campgrounds and recreational facilities near the water get the heaviest use. All recreationists, including boaters, have some negative environmental impact.

It is important that all hiker and campers attempt to minimize their impact. It is perhaps more important that recreationists organize to create more money and volunteer resources to help preserve and restore our wetlands and riverine environs.

Sportsmen have been doing this for well over sixty years. Nonsportsmen are sixty years behind the times. It's time the leaders of the Sierra Club, Audubon Society and other strong conservationist organizations recognize this critical failing of their programs and move to rectify it.

Fires

If you can do without a fire, do so. When you camp without a fire you will find that you see, hear and learn more about the world around you. Wildlife will come closer to your camp. You won't ruin your night vision by looking at the firelight. Since there won't be a fire to demand your attention, you will be more attentive to stars, the play of star and moon light on the world, and the intricate sounds of wind and animals. If you do build a fire, please keep the following in mind.

Don't build a fire ring. In fact, tear down every fire ring you see. The blackened rock stays forever as a sign that you once camped there. Build your fire on a fire lid (a metal trash can lid works great). Try to keep the lid from direct contact with the ground by setting it on a few small rocks.

Using a fire lid in this way prevents the fire from killing the plant roots in the soil. It also prevents the heat of the fire from carbonizing burnable material in the soil, thus preventing all the beaches turning into black polka dots.

Finally, since all your ashes will pretty much be on the lid, you can use the lid to carry the ashes to the creek and throw them into the current.

If you don't have a fire lid, dig a small pit to contain the fire. When you leave, you can use a cooking pot to scoop out the ashes, and put them into the current. After you smooth the area over with sand, the evidence of your fire will be minimal.

In riparian areas, try to locate your fire in sandy areas which are below the normal high water mark. This way, whatever evidence of a fire you do leave behind will disappear with the next regular cycle of high water.

Firewood

Be careful and considerate in your selection of firewood. Dead and decaying wood plays a very important role in the habitat, providing food and home for a wide variety of essential insects and birds. It provides shelter and staging areas for an even wider variety of reptiles, birds and mammals. As it rots, it revitalizes the soil to the benefit of the plants still alive.

Try to use driftwood exclusively for your fire. Even then, try to use that driftwood which has been left below the regular high water mark, since this wood would be moved away anyway. Driftwood left by the major, and rare, floods is helping to revitalize the soils of the higher elevation flood plains as it rots.

Trash

Refuse generated as a result of body elimination will be considered later. Take your cans, paper, plastic and Styrofoam® out with you.

Take somebody else's out with you also. There will always be selfish bastards who go to remote areas only to leave mounds of trash as evidence that they are worthless jerks. If you walk away from their failure, you join them.

Be particularly aware that tinfoil doesn't burn. Carry the individual packets of your hot chocolate out. Only the paper burns. The tinfoil stays. It's not just a visual issue here. Trash, especially plastics and fishing line, has been implicated in the deaths of various types of wildlife.

Some trash was not brought into the wild by the people directly. Floods pick up debris in the urban areas and carry it down. If you encounter large, heavy trash (like car tires) that you cannot rationally remove, try to help the river remove it. Move the tire, or whatever, out into the main force of the currents. As the floods come, it will be moved slowly and surely toward a final resting place in the mud flats of Horseshoe or Bartlett lakes.

Wildlife

It's not only the loud traveler who impacts wildlife. The fast traveler does also, especially if there are young present.

During the spring, move quietly and slowly when in the presence of animals with young. Bald eagles will abandon their nests if they get too much human disturbance. At least one biologist has suggested that river runners may be, in part, the reason for the low numbers of nesting mergansers along the Salt River.

Transportation

In most aspects of wilderness travel, boating causes the least amount of destruction, since trails are not created or made more permanent (I believe hikers call this increased permanence "improvements").

By far the most destructive form of transportation is anything wheeled, including mountain bikes. The real vicious damage is caused by vehicles with both wheels and motors. There is no imaginable reason why it is necessary to drive vehicles up and down the river.

Hikers and horsemen can take steps to minimize their impacts. If trails or roads exist, stay on them. Better yet, try to stay in the creek as much as possible, or at least below the regular high water mark.

Urination

It is best either to urinate in a very dispersed way (away from likely camping spots, or other places people will concentrate) or directly into the stream itself, **IF THE STREAM HAS SUFFICIENT FLOWS**.

Most Memorial Days for the past few years I have led a group of canoeists down the Wild and Scenic portion of the Verde to try to clear the trash. The campsites at Childs, Houston Creek, Red Creek and Sheep Crossing all have sections where the smell of human urine is clearly identifiable. Some folk use toilet paper after urination, which is a problem in itself. I will address it under defecation.

Defecation

When I lead the canoe crew down the Verde, I make sure we have along a sizeable supply of plastic medical examination gloves. We must clear most sites of toilet paper.

Eliminating bodily waste is a function that our society views as extraordinarily private. We lock the doors to the bathrooms. We flush the waste away. We spray perfumes into the air to conceal even the odors. Hell, we even employ a huge variety of euphemisms to refer to the facilities we use on such a regular basis.

Then, why, why, why do so many insist on leaving fluttering reminders marking the exact location you just got done using? Oh, I know. Toilet paper disintegrates in water, so the rains will get rid of it. **THIS IS THE DESERT!** We don't get lots of rain. That few, or not so few, sheets of paper is likely to stay there virtually unchanged for months, cheerfully fluttering out its undeniable message.

All over our remote areas are these little messages that this scat pile is human in nature. Toilet paper can be carried out, buried, or with a little bit of care and intelligence, burned.

The real kicker is that the very worst sites are the ones accessible (legally or illegally) by motorized vehicles. At Red Creek I have been able to clearly identify the limits of individual camping areas by noting the rings of toilet paper and feces, left as the campers crept as far from their own site, and as close to their neighbors, as possible.

Without spending much money, it is possible for these campers to create a secure, portable toilet that will maintain the environment, their privacy and increase their comfort.

Feces can be buried in a hole 100 feet or more from the stream. Better yet, if possible, take it out with you. Yes, I know. Cattle are leaving their feces in and very close to the water. Do you want to admit that you have all the environmental awareness of an animal bred for slaughter?

Portable Toilets

Buy one of the rectangular rocket boxes. Buy two if you want to have the Cadillac model. These are watertight in both directions.

In your rocket box you'll keep a goodly supply of large, sturdy trash bags and strong ties for them. Other supplies you will need (which may be in the second box if you have gone Cadillac) include toilet paper, some wood ashes or bleach (to fight gasses), hand soap or alcohol wipes, and some old toilet seat you have scarfed or reconstructed.

Don't urinate in the rocket box. Liquid is harder to contain in the box than a solid without breaking the plastic bag. After each round of defacation, put some wood ashes or bleach on the feces and toilet paper. At the end of each day, seal that day's worth of remains tightly, leave it in the box, and use a new bag the next day.

Keep the lid to the rocket box securely fastened when not in use. For each day on the river, you will have one sealed plastic bag with feces. The soap, toilet paper, tin can of water (for washing hands), or alcohol wipes can be kept, along with the toilet seat, near the toilet box. When you leave, the whole thing goes, safe and secure, with you. If you set up the Cadillac version, put all your supplies into the second rocket box, reserving the first rocket box for plastic bags with feces. The feces and paper can be dumped into some regular toilet. The used plastic bags can be bagged and sent out with your trash at home.

If you want privacy, you can create a screen with rope and ground cloths, or you can erect a tent which serves as your "bathroom." Some folk prefer a view to having privacy.

Successful descent is made at Punk Rock Rapid
at 100 cfs (Camp Verde).

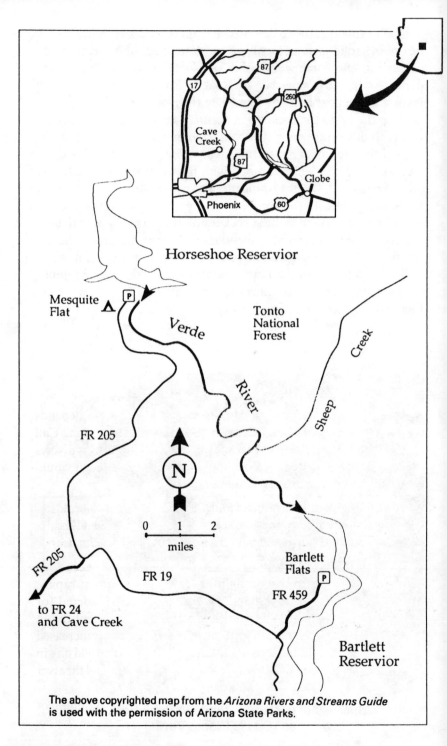

The above copyrighted map from the *Arizona Rivers and Streams Guide* is used with the permission of Arizona State Parks.

Horseshoe Dam to Bartlett Dam

Mileage: 20 miles

Elevation Change: 2000 to 1750

Warnings:
- Possible mud/sand flats at upper end of Bartlett Lake
- Impact of Driving Destroyers
- Nesting Bald Eagles
- Strainers just below Horseshoe Dam
- Flow dependent on wishes of Salt River Project

Motorized access:
- Numerous points off FR 205 and 262, just below Horseshoe Dam
- Mid point of Bartlett Lake using FR 459 and 459D
- Bartlett Dam, off FR 19

Days needed: One to two

Since this section is below a dam, the nature of the flow depends entirely on the wishes and needs of the Salt River Project. Call 236-5929 for current flows of that morning. (The recording is always there.) It is only updated on work days. Call 236-8888 if you would like to talk to a knowledgeable human being.

> The first mile or so is braided and, depending on which braids have water, could contain some very nasty strainers. If paddling, you may want to skip it and put on a mile or so downstream near the KA Ranch.

From here on the river is straightforward. No significant rapids, some small drops over rock bars. This section was considered for inclusion in the Federal Wild and Scenic Rivers system but didn't make the cut. Since it didn't, it also didn't get any increased protection. As a result, the Driving Destroyers have had a field day in the first part of this trip. Eventually, their impact dies out and the river is supported by isolated Sonoran desert.

This entire section shows the impact of dams. Expect a minimum of driftwood, since all driftwood would have to originate below

Horseshoe Dam. Bartlett Lake can start as high as four or five miles below Horseshoe Dam, depending on how much water is stored behind Bartlett Dam. There is often only eight miles or so of flowing water between Horseshoe Dam and the upper end of Bartlett Lake.

Bartlett Lake is a long, narrow affair and is rightly known as an angler's lake, though I prefer to fish Horseshoe Lake (less motorized stuff on the water).

The scenery is good all along this run, though. In the distance are Indian Butte, St. Clair Peak, and St. Clair Mt. (on the right). The second Canyon Creek you encounter is river left, as is SB Mountain and the Mazatzals.

I do not boat this much or hike it. That doesn't mean you should not. It is accessible and the shuttle is not difficult. It may be easy to find some friendly person willing to drop you off at Horseshoe , and go camp down by Bartlett to meet you at the next dam.

The fishing can be very good and there are catfish here big enough to swamp your boat. This would be a very good area to go into to see if you like boating the Verde. You are not obligated to be on the river long nor to travel great distances. While remote, it is not so isolated to make establishing contact with some other passerby an unreasonable expectation. This is a comforting thought, should you have difficulty on the water.

Bartlett Dam is at TRM 170.

Stable rock bars, such as the one on the left in photo
(river right on the river), often sport heavy plant growth.

Who Uses the River?

The Verde is a long river and a wide variety of folk use it. Some of these folk are on different points on a continuum and some seem to warrant their own special categories.

Motorized Campers—Driving Destroyers

Motorized campers drive in at some river access point and set up camp. Many of these campers are good, decent people who clean up after themselves and others. Most four-wheel drive enthusiasts who have organized into clubs belong to this category. These clubs often volunteer to help the Forest Service look after the more remote areas.

Driving Destroyers are dedicated to the idea that remote areas are improved by loud music, gunfire and heavy use of mind-altering substances. These poor critters often drive underpowered vehicles that have the capacity to carry full beer cans into the wilderness but can't get the empties out. When these folk are feeling real "in tune" with the land, they take their ORV's and scar everything in sight. Fortunately, many of them do not wear helmets. Over time, natural selection should remove them from the gene pool.

Day hikers—Backpackers

Day hikers are often boaters or motorized campers who are out for exploratory jaunts. Typically, they are found within a couple miles of their primary means of transportation.

Backpackers are good folk, whose idea of a good time is to sweat up and down a mountain.

Anglers

Some anglers (like me) are prone to sit by the bank, looking at the view, until some suicidal fish comes along and swallows the hook and bait. Other anglers actively pursue the fish with a variety of artificial devices made to imitate the natural stuff I put on my hook. This latter category of angler is a restless sort who usually knows more about the various species of fish than do the more laid-back anglers.

All anglers need to do a better job of cleaning up the debris left by slob anglers. Cast-off fish line has been implicated in the deaths of eagles and other fish predators.

Hunters

Some hunters are Driving Destroyers with guns. Others are the pillars of the conservationist movement. Hunters, more than any other group of outdoors folk, have self-organized to tax themselves to produce money for conservation and to produce volunteers for habitat improvement or to benefit select species.

Casual Boaters—Hardcore Paddlers

Casual Boaters are often motorized campers without the motors. Sometimes they are Driving Destroyers without motors (boat jargon for this subcategory is Float and Bloater). To both these subcategories, their boat is a means of transportation.

For Hardcore Paddlers (you wouldn't believe the teasing I get for participating in a sport where people are called hardcore paddlers and dress up in rubber) the boat takes on religious significance. These people talk about dancing with the river. Some of these paddlers only paddle peaceful, low-level water. Others only paddle the large rollercoaster stuff. Some paddle both. All are unified by a commitment to the experience of human-powered water craft.

Survivalists

Many of these people are hopelessly addicted to romantic notions of surviving in the wilderness while lacking the skills necessary to really give it a shot.

Outfitters

Boating outfitters and pack animal outfitters both provide a safe way for novices to experience the outback with minimal hardships and risks. Most outfitters do a good job of helping clean the mess left by others and in training their clients in appropriate outdoor ethics.

Birders

Hunters with binoculars. Usually found close to civilization.

Psychological Workers

There are some psychologist sorts out there convinced that they can reform disturbed juveniles by putting them into the wilderness for extended periods of time with limited supplies. Maybe they can.

This program is most likely to be encountered below Childs and during the winter.

Indians

The river does cross or pass near three different reservations.

Cowboys

Horses, cows, chaps, guns, spurs. I've always found these guys friendly.

Landowners

Mostly nice folk with tons of horror stories about the abuses they have suffered from Driving Destroyers and Float and Bloaters.

Potentially Dangerous Folk

I'm not lying here. Your chances of meeting any of these characters are slight. However, they do exist and they do exist along the Verde.

Potdiggers

Specializing in the destruction of our archaeological heritage for their own personal gain.

Potgrowers and Drug Smugglers

If by some remote and unlucky chance you find a pot field, or see a plane landing in some rugged wilderness area, don't investigate. Notify the authorities when you are safe at home.

Poachers and Rustlers

Poachers steal animals from the general public; rustlers steal from ranchers. Usually found near a road of some sort. Don't be nosey. Report your suspicions from the comfort of your home.

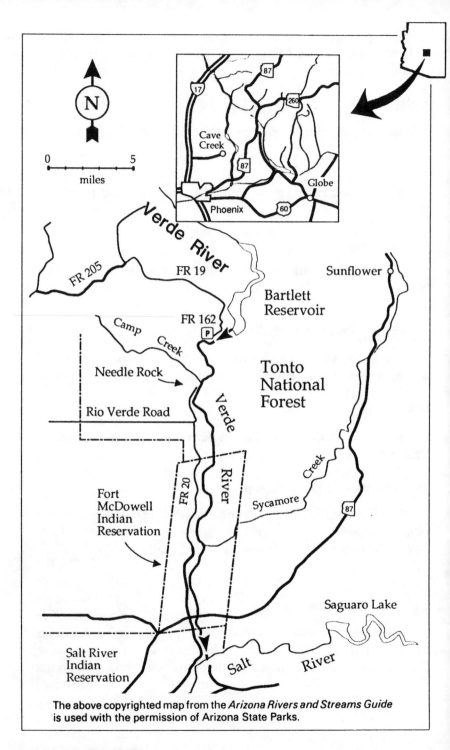

The above copyrighted map from the *Arizona Rivers and Streams Guide* is used with the permission of Arizona State Parks.

Bartlett Dam to Salt River

Mileage: 25 miles

Elevation Change: 1750 to 1320

Warnings:
- Private land
- Water dependent on dam release
- Reservation lands
- Driving Destroyer impact
- Float and Bloat impact
- Eagle closures

Motorized access:
- Bartlett Dam
- Multiple points below FR 162
- State Route 87 bridge
- Multiple points below Rt 87 bridge
- Phon D. Sutton Recreational Area (on Salt River, across from the mouth of the Verde

Days needed: One to two

When I boated this section, the SRP was allowing 450 cfs of water to escape below the dam. The entire trip took me about eight hours to complete. I traveled pretty much straight through, but I didn't paddle much, preferring to float. At lower flows, this section would take two days. I was only forced out of my boat by shallow water once. At significantly lower flows, a paddler would be out more often.

Visually, this section starts out quite attractively, though the Driving Destroyers have hit almost the entire 25 miles to one degree or another. The scenery below the dam is nice for seven miles or so. There are good views of mountains, cliffs, canyons, and streamside reeds. I particularly like the area where Bootleg Canyon enters a couple of miles below the dam.

Not far below the dam, you enter threatened and endangered species closures. Sometimes these closures apply to all recreationists, including boaters. Usually boaters are allowed to pass through, since it is possible for boaters to pass very quietly. The safest bet is to call the

Tonto Forest and ask if boaters are allowed to pass through, if you are going to try to boat this between January and June.

There are periodic areas appropriate for camping, usually on sand or pebble beaches. However, since all driftwood has to originate below Bartlett Dam, and since people drive into most of this area, firewood can be hard to find. The popularity with the motorized folk means you may have lots of company if you camp through here on a weekend night.

From the dam down past Needle Rock (also called Castle Rock), the scenery is Sonoran desert: saguaros, cholla and rough dry land. There is a natural arch at Needle Rock at TRM 176.75. A couple of years ago, AGFD was selling a beautiful poster of a pair of eagles circling each other by this spire.

Below Needle Rock, the country to the left flattens out. The right is a bit higher. Mesquite bosques (one of the rarest habitats in the US) dominate, but there are sections with cottonwoods. One of the most replenishing sections is about eight miles below the Dam, where a multitude of young cottonwood crowd each other. They are as thick as salt cedar.

For the next 10 to 12 miles virtually all elevated land is in the distance. What is close is all eroded flats and mesquite bosques. It is tempting to dismiss it as ugly, but that would be short-sighted. The area is packed with avian predators, especially herons and all sorts of raptors.

Because there are so few landmarks close to the river, it is easy to lose your place on a topo map through here. (I went right on past Fort McDowell before I realized it.) As you near the end of the journey, the journey of both you and the Verde itself, the McDowell Mountains stand off to the right. Pass under the Rt. 87 bridge, and watch Arizona Dam Butte and Mt. McDowell gradually increase in size. There is a recreation area just downstream and river right of this bridge.

The Verde tries to end with some style. Not more than one mile from the end is a fun rapid with some large rocks. At most levels it would be classed no higher than a 2. But it could be a Level 2 that would startle some beginning boaters. It isn't that difficult, but the large rocks can make it visually intimidating to some.

After this, you float quietly to the Salt. As you view the buildings of the filtration plant, you are seeing the end. The Verde (El Rio de Los Reyes) merges quietly with the Salt River. Across the Salt are some interesting boulders, and then the parking lot of the Phon D. Sutton recreation area. (Look for the T.V. antennas on the recreational vehicles.)

You are near the end of the Salt, also. Not three miles downstream, at 1,313 feet elevation, the Granite Reef diversion dam kills the entire river. Tamed, it is now sliced into small slivers and slipped into canals. The river bed remembers how it was created. It sits there, enduring the gravel pits and toxic waste dumps, until those rains come that overwhelm the two dams on the Verde and five on the Salt. Water, the old companion, then caresses the stream bed once again.

The Verde is gone. The Salt is gone. The river bed is dry. Dry until you get below the sewage treatment plants that process the wastes of millions of toilets. Then it flows with effluent, effluent of such poor quality that Arizona State Parks had to close Picture Rocks State Park because of the health hazard posed by the water. Fish taken from the water are feared unsafe and a danger to the low-income folk who eat them. It's an ignoble end to a flow of water that supports so much life and so much beauty upstream.

I couldn't watch the river succumb to its final slaughter. A river I have to share with other recreationists is better than no river at all. In another section of the book I've listed a number of conservationist organizations. Join one of them.

Riparian issues are often complex. It is only by joining one or more of the advocacy groups that you will be able to know when it is that you need to act.

The bow gets buried in Punk Rock Rapid at 100 cfs
(Camp Verde).

Chasing a fish lure after a bad cast.

Swimmer is in a bad spot. It's dangerous to be downstream of a swamped canoe.

What Are the Issues?
Who Are the Players?

Vegetation and Weather Control

Studies are now underway to investigate the feasibility of cloud seeding and eliminating some of the vegetation in the watershed in order to increase the amount of water which reaches the Phoenix metro area.

Minimum Stream Flow

Arizona has no laws guaranteeing that the streams of this state will continue to exist as ribbons of life. Desert riparian habitat is one of the rarest habitats in North America and the most productive habitat in the Southwest. All efforts to establish such standards, even on a limited site specific basis bring all sorts of protests.

Water Quality

The Center for Law in the Public Interest goes to court regularly to force responsible agencies to actually do their assigned jobs and protect the quality of our waters.

Recreation

I believe the development of a recreation industry based on stream-based recreation is the only way our streams will receive adequate protection. If we expect rural folk to help protect riparian zones, we are going to have to help create a situation where the protection of those zones is to the economic advantage of those who live near them.

Players in the Rivers Game

In writing this section, I have tried to avoid labeling good guys and bad guys. Those roles often change, depending on how the individual issues break.

Environmental Protection Agency

When they have the political courage, the EPA shuts down some of the operations savaging our riparian areas. When they don't have the courage, they can ignore dangerous levels of pollution in callous disregard of their legislated mission.

U.S. Forest Service

Most of the Verde River and its important tributaries are under control of the U.S. Forest Service. Many of the upper stations of other important drainages are under Forest Service control, also. By Congressional dictate, the Forest Service manages land for multiple use and sustained yield, while considering the relative values of the various resources.

The Service is also supposed to protect our historic, cultural and natural heritage. They do this by following plans which are developed every 10 to 15 years. All of this plan development and implementation is done under the scrutiny of large and powerful special interests.

Those who purport to care about rivers should become members of one or more of these special-interest groups. Leaders of these groups should recognize that the economic impact of recreational use needs to be quantified.

Bureau of Land Management

The BLM does not control any aspect of the Verde. However, they do control important aspects of about 11 percent of our perennial streams.

National Park Service

Tuzigoot, Montezuma Well and Montezuma Castle Monuments are all in the Verde watershed.

U.S. Fish and Wildlife Service

This service manages a number of wildlife refuges located in Arizona, but not in the Verde watershed. The service is also involved in addressing issues surrounding Threatened and Endangered species, making them a noteworthy player in the Verde.

Bureau of Reclamation

Most of our dams and the Central Arizona Project were constructed under the supervision of these folk.

Recently, they have been active in the Arizona Riparian Council to help lay the groundwork for measuring and granting minimum stream flows.

What can I say? The Bureau has a long history of slaughtering riparian areas. Perhaps they are now moving toward a more productive role?

Indian Reservations

The tribes operate with a great deal of autonomy from the state and federal resource management folk. Some of the tribes are major players on some of our drainages. The tribes along the Verde have not, at this point, initiated highly restrictive regulations. It is not possible to generalize about the tribes as a whole since they vary in their approach to recreation and economic development.

Arizona Outdoor Recreation Coordination Commission

This Commission makes the recommendations for the spending of State Lake Improvement Funds (SLIF). These monies are derived from taxes on boats and gasoline for boats. The money is to be spent developing water-based recreation. In recent years, some of the money has been targeted for developing recreation sites along rivers as well as along lakes.

Arizona Commission on the Environment

This Commission makes recommendations to the leaders of our state on environmental issues. They help arrange meetings and seminars of those interested in environmental issues.

Salt River Project

These folk administer many of the dams built by the Bureau of Reclamation. The SRP provides irrigation water to the Phoenix metro area. They control releases from Horseshoe and Bartlett dams.

Now active in the Arizona Riparian Council, they provide the public service of a telephone number that gives the daily cfs flows on sections of various rivers.

Arizona Game and Fish Department

Responsible for the management of fish and wildlife throughout the state, except on Indian Reservations. The positions of the Department and the governing Commission often serve as rallying points for sportsmen concerned with riparian issues. This Department receives no general tax revenue. It is supported entirely by voluntary donations, license fees, excise taxes levied on hunting and fishing equipment, and the Heritage Fund.

Arizona Department of Environmental Quality

Responsible for setting, monitoring and enforcing water quality standards for all navigable waters, their tributaries and our groundwater.

Arizona Department of Water Resources

They have authority over the appropriation and distribution of waters in Arizona. They have control over streams, dams, reservoirs, irrigation districts, flood control, weather control, cloud modification, and vegetation modification. They have the responsibility for issuing grants of minimum instream flow rights.

Arizona State Land Department

Holds and operates a large amount of acreage in trust to benefit Arizona public education. In order to fulfill its mandated charge to generate money for schools while not participating in continuing genocide of our riparian areas, this department tries to exchange lands it holds that have high riparian values with BLM for properties with high commercial value.

Arizona State Parks

Owns and operates Dead Horse Ranch State Park. They are very active on Verde River issues.

County and Local Governments

Some follow a strict policy of encouraging their residents to grow desert plants and otherwise acknowledge the fact that we live in a desert. Others don't.

In 1988, Tucson residents used an average of 164 gallons of water per person per day. Phoenix residents used 253. Scottsdale residents consumed 316 gallons. The denizens of Paradise Valley employed 862 gallons of water per person per day.

Private Players

The following organizations are largely driven by volunteers. They vary tremendously in their effectiveness and by the extent to which they rely on paid staff to represent them.

Arizona Riparian Council

Dominated by academics from the universities, the agencies, and the Nature Conservancy. Address is ASU, Center for Environmental Studies, Arizona Riparian Council, Tempe, AZ 85287. The newsletter is informative and tracks what is going on with the agencies.

The Nature Conservancy

Dedicated to the private and corporate raising of funds to purchase lands to protect threatened and endangered life forms. Address is 300 East University Blvd., Suite 230, Tucson, AZ 85705.

Northern Arizona Paddlers Club

Small club. When aroused, they have shown the ability to have influence way beyond what their numbers would indicate. Address is P.O. Box 1224, Flagstaff, AZ 86002.

Central Arizona Paddlers Club

Younger than the Northern Arizona Paddlers. They were involved and effective in the rivers and stream study of the SCORP. Does volunteer work for the Forest Service. Address is P.O. Box 11090, Suite 374, Phoenix, AZ 85061.

Anglers United

A warm water anglers organization which raises funds and does volunteer labor for AGFD. Address is 730 N. Robson Road, Mesa, AZ 85201.

Center for Law in the Public Interest

Address is 3208 East Ft. Lowell, #106, Tucson, AZ 85116. They file innumerable court actions to protect the "public" interest on behalf of rivers and water issues.

Sierra Club

Address is 3201 N. 16th St., #6A, Phoenix, AZ 85016. This address can steer you to the Sierra Club group that represents members in your geographic area. The affiliation with a national organization can be very helpful at times.

Arizona Wildlife Federation

A collection of conservationist organizations, mostly of a sportsman's bent. They are active on AGFD, Forest Service and BLM issues, and sponsor periodic volunteer projects. Many of their affiliated clubs deserve to be mentioned here in their own right. The affiliation with the National Wildlife Federation is often useful. Address is 644 N. Country Club Drive, Suite E, Mesa, Arizona 85201.

Tucson Rod and Gun Club

Address is P.O. Box 12921, Tucson, AZ 85732. Very active with the agencies and at the legislature. Holds periodic volunteer work projects. This club has been a committed and productive supporter of the AGFD Native Fish Program. They also operate a firing range in Tucson.

Maricopa Audubon

Very active with agencies and legislature. These folk write a host of articles that end up being published by both the AWF and the Sierra Club. Address is 4735 N. 53rd St., Phoenix, AZ 85018.

Trout Unlimited

Raises funds and organizes conservationist projects. Address is 3633 W. Gardenia Ave., Phoenix, AZ 85051.

Friends of Arizona Rivers

Active on all issues that impact Arizona rivers. Address is 1915 West Hazelwood Parkway, Phoenix, AZ 85015.

Working hard at 50 cfs (Camp Verde).

Relaxing and allowing the current to do the work.

Summer heat is not much of a problem to canoeists.

A solo canoeist usually has an easier time than tandem canoeists with vertical drops.

Tributaries

Sycamore Canyon (#1)

A number of Sycamore Creeks join the Verde. The most spectacular is the one which merges with the Verde at Packard Ranch.

This creek will never be of much interest to boaters, as the stream is intermittent and there is no rational upstream access for boaters. Hikers are a different matter. Sycamore Creek and the canyon that cradles it are located in a federally-designated wilderness area. The lower canyon reaches depths of 1000 feet. If you understand topo maps, buy the 15-minute Clarkdale quad. It will immediately let you know what the area of Sycamore Canyon and the nearby gorge on the Verde below Perkinsville are all about.

Trailheads to the lower canyon are reached by taking the turnout of Clarkdale toward the Tuzigoot Monument. Immediately after crossing the Verde, take the dirt road to the west. Follow it some eight miles or so to its end. That is the parking lot and access point for hikes up the lower canyon.

If you are interested in access to the upper creek, near Garland Prairie, buy a Coconino Forest map, figure out which Forest Roads or trails interest you, and then call the Coconino Forest to get detailed information. Just because a road or trail shows on a map does not mean it is passable or open to use. It doesn't even guarantee that it exists. It's always a good idea to have a topo map of the area.

Oak Creek

This is the largest and best-known tributary of the Verde. All of Oak Creek has been boated, some of it at flood levels. Few of you will ever boat any section above Page Springs. Most of you will boat it only below Cornville.

Above State Rt. 179

Oak Creek starts above Sedona where Sterling Canyon, Sterling Spring and Pumphouse Wash all come together. For the next 16 miles, Oak Creek rolls to Sedona, gathering water from tribs such as West Fork Oak Creek, and numerous springs, as well as from rainwater or snowmelt which rushes down the washes off the Mogollon Rim.

(Incidentally, just on the river left side of Rt. 179, another road joins 179 from the north. This is the bottom end of Schnebley Hill Road. This road makes a spectacular (dirt) climb up over the cliffs that make up the bottom end of Oak Creek Canyon. It is one of the most beautiful dirt roads in the state. It joins with Interstate 17 twenty miles or so south of Flagstaff. It is prettier to drive it downhill. **It becomes impassable in snow, snowmelt or heavy rains**).

Oak Creek Canyon is one of the most photographed places in Arizona. Tourists crowd into it to swim, hike, golf, luxuriate, ride on jeep tours, and fish for hatchery-stocked trout. The place often gets very, very crowded. That beautiful clear water can contain sewage from nearby homes and resorts. A new sewage system which is going in may solve this. However, it won't deal with the sewage which is contributed by too many children with insufficient bowel control at Slide Rock. Almost all of this area is in public lands and is open to the public. Camping is tightly restricted.

When this section has sufficient water to boat, it is the property of only highly-skilled boaters. There are some **very steep drops**. Strainers are omnipresent. Resting eddies are rare.

Sedona to Page Springs (14 to 15 miles)

Speed of the elevation drop moderates. Some very steep drops and steep rock-strewn drops still exist, especially below the YMCA camp. Below Red Rock Crossing the houses drop off sharply and a sense of isolation returns. I have boated this at moderately high water and found sections of it real attention-getting. At moderately high flow it is a fun-challenging trip for a boater who is already comfortable with the Beasley Flats to Childs section of the Verde at levels of 500 cfs (Camp Verde) or higher.

Page Springs to Cornville (8 miles)

In this section the river sits in a series of entrenched meanders caused by the continuing uplift of the Verde Valley. At reasonably high flows, this is a Class 2 section of the creek. **Dangerous strainers** are possible herein, as they always are along any section of any creek that is tree-lined.

The only gauge is a visual guess made by looking at the bridge abutments at Page Spring. Stand on the river right bank and look across to the river left. Pick out the second concrete pad from the left which has water flowing around it. If the water is flowing over the top of the upstream end of that footing, there is enough water to canoe down to Cornville.

Some of this section is through floodplain, with beautiful large trees. Some of the time the river flows past banks stabilized with rusting car bodies. There are many houses and much private property.

Cornville to the Verde River (7 miles)

Just below Cornville the creek environs change dramatically. The creek, still in its entrenched meanders, flows through open, deserty land. There are few homes and usually few people. This is a Class 1 trip. It always has enough water for those of you in plastic canoes who travel very light. It is a good canoe trip to chase bass or trout. Put in at the Cornville Bridge. Take out at Sheep Crossing or Bignott Beach. Give it a try. It is a nice trip!

Beaver Creek(s)

Beaver Creek, along with Wet and Dry Beaver Creeks, are some pretty incredible drainages. All drain the Mogollon Rim. I will start with Wet Beaver, since it is perennial.

Wet Beaver Headwaters to Confluence with Dry Beaver

Wet Beaver starts high on the Mogollon Rim, near Apache Maid Mountain, where it is heavily treed and populated with squirrels. Upper Wet Beaver is noted in the AGFD book *Arizona Tree Squirrels* as being good habitat for fox squirrels. If you are interested in exploring this upper end, do some research, then call the Coconino Forest. Many of the "roads" are better fit for horses than motorized vehicles.

Shortly, the creek dives over the Rim, cutting a deep and beautiful canyon that is both wilderness and Wilderness. For eight to nine miles the creek is a series of deep and shallow pools separated by rocky drops nestled in a deep and narrow canyon.

Often the deep pools reach canyon wall to canyon wall, requiring the would-be hiker to bring along flotation in order to swim/float across the pools. There are fish in these waters and I consider the pool just up river of Bell's Crossing to be one of the best swimming holes in the universe.

I did learn a very important lesson about flash floods here. Years ago, a friend and I decided to go backpacking up in the Wet Beaver Creek area between Christmas and New Year. There had been a lot of moisture that year and the snow pack up on the Mogollon Rim was two feet or more thick. A storm front moved in bringing with it warm rains. In deference to the weather, we decided that we would only hike into Bell Crossing, set up base camp, and do day hikes.

We hiked in and established camp. It rained all day and all night. The next day, we got up and, stepping across the stones in the shallow creek, hiked up into the newly-created wilderness area.

We were in rough and wild country, beautiful in the wet and low clouds. We played half the day and returned to camp for lunch.

The sound of the ripples at the crossing suddenly changed. Looking down, we saw that the clear water had gone brown, and was starting to rise at an extraordinarily fast rate.

Fifteen minutes later the little creek had picked up six to seven vertical feet of water. Tree trunks were being tossed down the river and up against the inner gorge walls. There was a constant roar and rumble as the water tore the boulders out of the stream bed and sent them crashing downstream.

Hours later, when we decided to hike out, the stream was still not crossable. Twenty minutes before the flood came down, we had been on the wrong side with virtually no gear. At least, we had not hiked up creek into the area of sheer walls.

We were badly shaken. It was clear we had entered the situation with wholly inadequate appreciation for the risks. We had run potentially lethal risks with ignorant smiles.

The trail was intact, having been built high above the creek. We had views of the cold muddy water tearing through the landscape that I still visualize today.

We got to our car the same time as the rangers. They were going to leave a note asking us to make sure to check in before we left. They were glad to see us. We were glad to see them. At our respective homes that night, we turned on the news. The flood wasn't mentioned. It was no big deal.

There is a ranger station and campground on Wet Beaver. Large sycamores and other trees give it an eastern feel. There is another swimming hole near the campground. You can get into here by taking FR 618 east at the Rt. 179 exit off I-17.

> Below the campground the creek picks up something of a flood plain and a whole lot of trees. A friend and I canoed from the Ranger Station to the Verde River one high water day. **I do not recommend it for anyone other than advanced or high intermediate paddlers.** There are some very, very steep rock bars. Some of the drops occur on blind curves and/or smack up against cliffs. The area is heavily treed and there are trees growing in the creek bed itself.

Strainers are an ever-present danger. On this particular trip we did wrap the canoe around an underwater stump. It was only the presence of a bow saw that saved us from a walk out. After a bit, the drop does moderate and houses and fences appear. You paddle past the beautiful and peaceful Montezuma Well to where the Wet Beaver joins the Dry Beaver at McGuireville. This is also the site of another gravel pit.

While I can't recommend this section to any but highly-skilled paddlers, it is a nice area to hike in. There is a good bit of wildlife, including beavers, beaver dams, black hawks and other forest critters. My wife, Beth, went to explore a rustling in a driftwood pile only to discover a skunk who stamped out a defiant message of annoyance.

Dry Beaver Headwaters to McGuireville

Headwaters ia a misnomer. Throughout most of its length, Dry Beaver carries water only during times of runoff. High on the Rim, Woods Canyon (which flows under I-17), Rattlesnake Canyon (which flows under I-17), and Horse Canyon come together to form Dry Beaver. Dry Beaver cuts down toward Sedona, and Jacks Canyon joins it just before Dry Beaver passes underneath State Route 179. Hikers can pick up trail #93 here which follows Dry Beaver and Wood Canyon. Connections can be made to hike trail #94 which ascends Horse Canyon.

Give this hike some time, but don't bother boating it. The creek bed has lots of trees growing in it. About the time you have enough flow to boat, you have enough push to wrap you up in the living strainers. Above 179 the area is Wilderness. Below, it is just remote. About midway between 179 and McGuireville is a small water falls. I know of some local boaters who drive up to here from below when the water flows and run the falls again and again.

I ran this once, I doubt I'll repeat. If I want to do something small and exciting, I'll do Wet Beaver.

Beaver Creek - Wet/Dry Confluence to Montezuma Castle

At the joining of Wet and Dry, the creek becomes known simply as Beaver Creek. Virtually all this land in here is private. **I can't recommend it for boaters** for some of the same reasons I don't recommend Wet Beaver. While the strainers are not omnipresent here, they occur with sufficient frequency to be a **real hazard** to the novice or careless boater.

Montezuma Castle to Verde River

Montezuma Castle is the put in. It's nice to have a National Monument as a put in. There are warm restrooms in which to put on your wet suit. The Castle itself is a Sinagua ruin. It is a beautiful spot with a picnic area and lots of sycamores.

Spend some time here to sit on the benches and look at the land. Feel the difference in moisture and temperature, as compared to the higher country nearby.

Boaters get great views of the ruins once on the creek, if you turn and look upstream. When this section is flowing, it is one of the nicest day trips in the Verde Valley for a boater. Short, only six or so miles by creek, with a shuttle drive that takes mere minutes. If there is sufficient water at the Castle itself to rationally paddle a canoe, there is sufficient water for the entire trip.

For the first four miles you paddle past limestone cliffs and some of the biggest sycamore trees I have ever seen (up to six feet in diameter). I've seen owls more than once on the limestone cliffs.

As you near Camp Verde, there is some deterioration of scenery. There are a couple of diversion dams or low water crossings made of car bodies and I have seen cables in the water below one of them. **I'm always careful if I choose to run any man-made obstruction.**

The creek joins the Verde 50 yards or so below where the Middle Verde-Camp Verde road crosses the Verde. This bridge serves as a motorized access spot. It may also be possible to paddle down the Verde a bit and take out river right on a cottonwood bench below the River Caves estates.

As you near the Verde, you paddle past the site of the long abandoned Fort Lincoln.

West Clear Creek

Take what I said about Wet Beaver above Bell's Crossing and intensify it. This drainage is a wonder. The bottom few miles have Forest Service campgrounds and some private homes. The extensive drainage up river is remote, wild and such a rush to experience.

Way up on the Rim, Clover Creek and Willow Valley Spring join to form West Clear Creek. (East Clear Creek flows into the Little Colorado and is a beautiful creek in itself.) Shortly, the creek slices the Mogollon Rim, creating a long, deep canyon through roadless area. The Creek is close to 30 miles long. Most of it is roadless. Almost one-half of it is trailless. There is a wide variety of possible access at the upper end. Call the Coconino Forest for information.

As with Wet Beaver, much of West Clear is located within an inner gorge wherein deep pools of water are sandwiched between sheer cliff walls. This is no place for the unprepared or inexperienced. **It is no place for anyone whenever a flash flood is remotely possible.**

Many folk use trail 17 to walk in at the Bull Pen Ranch or restrict themselves to the campground area near FR 618. There is access off trail 17 at a point six or so miles above the Bull Pen. Hike down off FR 214. This is near where the deep pools begin.

Sycamore Creek (#2)

A lovely little canyon. It enters the Verde at a downstream angle while you are occupied with a long stretch of Class 2 water, so it is easy to miss. Forest maps do not show it as having perennial water. There are lots of springs in the canyon so there are sections with constant water.

This canyon defines the downstream boundary of a nesting eagle closure. Between January and June you are being friendly and polite to the eagles if you go downstream to the bottom of the rapids before stopping to rest or picnic.

As you drive into Childs on FR 708 you cross the upper end of this. It is often wet and green.

Gap Creek

This drainage starts high on Tule Mesa and Tule Mountain. The upper sections are in rough isolated terrain. AGFD has restocked a population of Arizona's only native trout species here. You might be able to get here using trail 163. Call the Verde District Office of Prescott Forest for details.

Gap Creek (or at least the drainage, as the stream is intermittent) travels past the Brown Ranch and Brown Springs. This lower section periodically suffers from illegal use by the Driving Destroyers who come in off FR 574.

The drainage joins the Verde below Punk Rock Rapid and above Bushman Rapid.

Fossil Creek

This drainage starts northwest of Strawberry. It is very rugged and beautiful country, isolated, except for the dirt road (FR 154) from Childs to Strawberry. This is a beautiful road, more scenic than the road from Childs to Camp Verde.

Fossil Springs, located a few miles from the Irving power plant, once dumped 20,000 gallons a minute into this drainage. No more. This water is taken out of the drainage (after being used to power the

Irving power plant) and is funneled down to power the Childs power plant. This arrangement is now being applauded as environmentally sound.

What water remains in the creek (sections are perennial), flows past Deadman Mesa until turned by Ike's Backbone. It joins the Verde just after Hardscrapple Creek dumps into Fossil Creek. It joins the Verde at a downstream angle just above Nasty Little Dogleg Rapid, which it created with its outflow.

There is good, though rough, hiking herein. Parts of the drainage are easily accessible off FR 502 into Childs.

East Verde River

The East Verde has an unnatural water flow. In the early 1960s, Phelps Dodge needed more water in Morenci for its mining operations. The problem was most of the water rights in that area belonged to the SRP.

Phelps Dodge acquired water rights to water from East Clear Creek, which is part of the Little Colorado River drainage. Phelps Dodge then built the Blue Ridge Reservoir to store their water. The arrangement with SRP allowed PD to take SRP water from the Black River in the Salt River drainage. In return, PD agreed to pump an equal amount of East Clear Creek water over nine miles into the East Verde River, which is in the Salt River Drainage.

PD stores water in the reservoir during the winter, pumping it down the East Verde in the summer.

The East Verde drainage begins miles and miles northeast of Payson, up under the Mogollon Rim, near Battleground Ridge. There is a marker commemorating the Battle of Big Dry Wash just off FR 705. The upper end is heavily used for recreation, especially near where it flows underneath State Route 87. FR 32 and 199 can also be used to explore the upper section of the river.

West of Payson it enters the Mazatzal Wilderness and begins to flow to the northwest. **Deep, deep, and rugged canyons** reward those who explore. **This is no place for beginners of any sort.**

The East Verde joins the Verde shortly below Fossil Creek. A trail comes very close to this juncture and the land where the two rivers join is a popular camping area. The fishing is excellent at that point, as it tends to be wherever two streams join.

Houston Creek

Houston begins high on Tule Mesa, near Tule Mountain, very near to the headwaters of Gap Creek. Houston Creek chooses to flow southeast, where it crosses FR 16. Below here it enters Wilderness, though Driving Destroyers often violate the sanctity of the area.

It joins the Verde a mile below the East Verde, at one of the most predictably trashed sites along this wonderful river. Just below this confluence is Squaw Butte.

Canyon Creek (#1)

Canyon Creek and a number of other small creeks join the Verde near Canoe Mesa. There are lots of springs in the area and the area is a good one to go exploring. It is accessible by using trails 12, 20 and 34.

Red Creek

Comes to life up in the Pine Mountain Wilderness, near Mockingbird Pass. FR 39 provides the closest access. As it descends, it gathers the Middle Red and North Red Creek drainages.

It is legal to drive to the Verde at this point. Driving Destroyers do so, along with considerate motorized campers. Access is down FR 18. The Forest Maps don't show this road going the whole way to Red Creek, but people regularly make connections to the river by using this road.

This site is usually the second most heavily trashed on the river after the Memorial Day weekend. The joining of the Red and Verde has produced trees and grass. It has a deep pool which can produce catfish 15 pounds or more. I understand why people come here. I just wish they would take their crap (figuratively and literally) when they leave. The fact that a four-wheel-drive club has agreed to help look after this place should help immensely.

Tangle Creek

Tangle starts north of West Cedar Mountain and flows southeast between East Cedar Mountain and Tangle Peak. It is crossed by FR 269 as the road winds its way toward Sheep Bridge. This is a good area for walking or hiking. The mouth of Tangle Creek, which creates a fairly long rapid and a few islands, is walking distance upstream from Sheep Bridge.

Upriver of this rapid is one of the most beautiful pool on the entire Verde. Reddish rocks and heavy growths of reeds create a magical effect.

Sycamore Creek (#3)

The third Sycamore Creek to join the Verde is dry at the confluence near Sheep Bridge. There is perennial water upstream. There is no trail up the drainage. Trail 22 can be used to get nearby.

Horse Canyon

Trail 223, the Willow Springs Trail, will take you up this drainage. Trailhead is at Sheep Bridge.

Canyon Creek (#2)

This Canyon Creek is better known than its little upstream brother. Its confluence with the Verde is buried under the waters of Bartlett Lake. It is possible to visit the upper end of the creek using Trail 87 or 92. The closest Forest Road is 393.

Sycamore Creek (#4)

Upstream access is FR 22, Bushnell Tank Road, off SR 87. The upper end is dominated by sycamores, the lower end by willows and off-road vehicles.

That's Not All

These are not the only drainages with perennial water that join the Verde, nor are all the beautiful canyons mentioned here. Using the appropriate Forest and topo maps, you're sure to find an isolated spot of green trees and quiet pools.

Boating Advice

Law and Boaters

The question "Who owns the land between the natural high water marks?" has plagued Arizona since 1985, when a State's Attorney claimed state ownership of the Verde River in a dispute with a gravel operation. Prior to that, streambed land was bought and sold for generations, in blissful ignorance of federal law which gives the state ownership to all lands below the highwater mark of all streams which were navigable at the time Arizona entered the Union. Immediately, the validity of deeds to over 40,000 parcels of land were thrown into doubt.

In 1986 the legislature passed a bill which allowed landowners to buy quit claims of streambed land from the state for a price per acre dramatically below market value. This same law gave boaters specific rights to passage to the Verde, Gila, and Salt Rivers. The Center for Law in the Public Interest took the state to court alleging that this issuance of quit claims violated the Arizona Constitution. (I was deposed by the parties involved in this case and spent over 5 hours being grilled by 7 attorneys.)

The arguments of the Center for Law were supported by legal briefs from virtually all the states in the western United States, except Arizona. In 1991 the Arizona Court of Appeals decided in favor of the Center and overturned the law. The legislature took up the problem in the 1992 legislature and passed House Bill 2594, which amended several statutes to try to fix the problem. This bill repealed the actions passed in 1986, including the specific mentioned rights of boaters for downstream access.

The new laws establish the Navigable Stream Adjudication commission through July 1, 2000. The members of the Commission are appointed by the Governor. This Commission is to look at all contested lands, determine whether the relevant streams were navigable at time of statehood, and determine the various relevant public values (habitat, recreation, etc.). If it is determined that the state has no legitimate claim to the land, that decision amounts to an abandonment of any state interest in that land (subject to court challenge). If it is determined that the state does have a legitimate claim, the Commission will then compile the list of public interests. The State Land Commissioner will then compare the advantages of keeping the land in state ownership to selling or renting it to the private sector at market value. In either case, the public interests must be protected. The Commissioner may also enter negotiations with a private person/corporation with a claim to a piece of property with an unclear history of navigability, and offer to surrender state claim to ownership in return for an agreement protecting the relevant public interests. All of this must be done under the light of public hearings and comment.

So, where does this leave boaters, other recreationists and the ability of the state to protect riparian habitat?

The repealed laws guaranteed downstream passage to the Salt, Gila, and Verde but to no other streams. Under the new law, all KNOWN public interests (including but not limited to downstream boater access) to ALL streams which were NAVIGABLE AT THE TIME OF STATE-HOOD must be protected by the state. Also, there is an Arizona statute which lists recreation as an appropriate and protected activity within Arizona. (I have heard rural, very conservative law officers in Arizona assert their belief that any downstream passage within the waters of a flowing stream is legally protected.) My belief is that the downstream passage for boaters is safe at least on the Salt, Gila, Verde, San Francisco, Oak, Beaver, Virgin, San Pedro, Blue, and Bill Williams as well as for sections of rivers such as the Little Colorado, Santa Cruz, East Verde, East Clear Creek, the Black, the White, Wet Beaver, and West Clear. (These lists are meant to serve as samples and NOT as the entire listing of rivers of which all or part could be under state ownership.)

This law should also increase the rights of other recreationists (such as horsemen, anglers, hunters, and hikers) as well as the ability of the state to protect habitat, on those streams and stream sections where the state asserts a claim to a particular stream or stream section.

Remember, the Commission (whose decisions are subject to court review) must consider all KNOWN PUBLIC VALUES CONNECTED WITH THOSE STREAMS WHICH WERE NAVIGABLE AT THE TIME ARIZONA ENTERED THE UNION. The knowledge of all individuals, groups, clubs, and agencies concerning public values connected to streams which may have been navigable at statehood should be made available to this Commission. Personal records, recreational business and club records, or newsletters on activities within riparian zones, or on habitat values, are relevant. The way to be informed is to write the State Land Commissioner and request to be kept informed on proposed actions, hearings, and determinations concerning streambed lands under ARS 37-1126.B, 37-1127.B, 37-1128.B, 37-1151.B, 37-1153.B and 37-1154.C.

If there are particular streams in which you have an interest, mention them specifically. All recreationists, conservationists, and associated clubs should do this to help create a listing of the public interests associated with their particular interests. Also, write the Center for Law in the Public Interest and let them know the streams on which you possess specific information.

Boaters have a specific and heavy obligation. The only lands to which state claims can be made are those which were navigable at the time of statehood. Consider this:

—A stream could have been NAVIGABLE at statehood even if it has not been proven to have been navigated at statehood.

—A stream need not be navigable year-round to qualify as navigable.

—If a stream was navigable, but human interference through dams, diversions, or overpumping took away the water flow, the stream is still considered navigable for the purposes of establishing state claim to the land.

—The existence of nonnavigable sections, due to rapids, falls, waterless sections, or other natural occurrences does not render the stream as a whole nonnavigable for the purpose of asserting a state claim.

—There have been decisions in other states which uphold the idea that a stream which was not navigable at time of statehood, but by using the technology of today is navigable, became valid reason for the purpose of asserting state claim to the lands.

Boaters, paddler clubs, and paddler magazines SHOULD NOT say or infer that a stream is unboatable if what they mean is the stream is too low, or high, or rough, or flat or tree-lined for their particular paddling tastes. Such comments could find their way into the commission or court as evidence that a stream has minimal public value, or was not navigable at statehood. Also, go paddle small streams and keep careful records of dates and conditions. Finally, don't forget to write the state land commissioner and let him know you possess information relating to the issue of stream navigability and/or public values.

None of us can let our individual and group responsibilities drop on this. It is the boaters, (past, present, and future) who hold the responsibility to secure the beachhead for the coming fight. All share in the fight to see that all public interests are known and protected.

We have the opportunity to protect habitat and provide access only as long as we grasp our individual, club, and business responsibilities.

Why Boat Shallow Water?

Some boaters are only interested in hydraulic thrill. They would rather boat Class 3 water located in a cement ditch than Class 1 water in a beautiful canyon. I do like heavy water, but my deepest attraction is for the riparian habitat.

Canoes, and other human-powered boats can be used as a pack animal, as a means of hauling humans and gear into remote areas. While boats are restricted to watery trails, they have numerous advantages over pack animals. They are less expensive to buy, feed and house. Vet bills are a rarity. They do not eat the riparian growth or defecate on the beach.

When deciding whether a section of creek is worth canoeing, I look at the effort it would take to gain the same access by backpacking. For example, let's say that a section of creek is 20 miles long. Over that 20 miles let's say that I will be out of my boat, dragging over wet rocks or simply wading beside my boat, for a total of a mile. Let's also say that that mile is broken into sections of four yards here, 15 yards there, and 40 yards over there. So, for one mile I'm out of my boat, and for 19 miles the boat carries me and my gear. Sounds like a fair deal to me.

I believe plastic canoes are the best single craft to have. They do not conduct heat or cold very well, they are durable, and they slide easily off rocks. Touching a metal boat in the dead of winter or in the heat of summer is not fun. Metal, wood and fiberglass all lack the durability necessary to boat shallow creeks. None of the latter materials will slide off rocks as well as does plastic.

Coleman canoes are the least expensive and most widely available plastic canoe. It is easy to find a used Coleman for sale. Colemans are durable but they come with an internal metal skeleton that can resemble a train wreck if you wrap your boat. Colemans are a good choice for folk on a tight budget, or as someone's first canoe.

Those who become enmeshed in the sport of canoeing almost always graduate to some more expensive canoe of a design more specific to the type of paddling they intend to do. There is a large variety of "name" canoes sold in Arizona. Dagger, Old Town, Blue Hole, Mohawk and Mad River canoes are all available in Arizona and are all manufactured by quality companies.

Kayaks and decked canoes are craft built not to ship water when exposed to large waves and turbulence. They are used in whitewater and on large lakes or bodies of salt water. The amount of gear you can take is limited and the paddler has no real choice of body position. A properly designed open canoe in the hands of a competent paddler can go anywhere these decked boats can.

Rafts and inflatable kayaks range from cheap to expensive. Use the cheap ones in a swimming pool. They are too fragile for stream boating. The expensive ones are durable and easy to learn to paddle. However, they do not slide as easily over rocks and it is ill-advised to use them to carry heavy rocket boxes.

Paddling With Loved Ones

When I teach beginners to canoe, I try to initially separate parents from children and separate romantically-involved adults. There seems to be something about humans being emotionally close to each other that convinces us that we need not show the other person any patience or courtesy. If you do find yourself taking loved ones out on the river, I have some suggestions.

1. Don't fight. It's not worth it. You will never convince your loved ones that this activity is something they want to do if—whenever they do it—you yell at them.

2. Don't demean their efforts, especially if you are better at the activity than they are. You were pretty incompetent once yourself.

3. Make it your number one priority that they have a good time. When I was teaching my wife to canoe, we would only boat in warm pleasant weather. I would insist that she bring a book, a little wine. I would offer to slowly guide the craft while she imitated Cleopatra. As she decided that she wanted to paddle more challenging water, I never criticized mistakes. As she wanted instruction, I met her request.

Eventually, when she decided that my willingness to do this sport in conditions that required dressing up in rubber suits was too weird for her to join me, I didn't press her to go. As a result, she doesn't discourage me from going.

4. Your kids absolutely have the power to make your trip miserable. Plan for their limitations and wishes. If they are having fun, they will tolerate more, more cheerfully. If you are traveling with young kids, plan short trips and short days. Add lots of sand castles, swimming, bug chasing and fishing.

5. When what you want is a serious hard-core trip, find like-minded travelers. Don't try to force it on those emotionally close to you.

6. Give your kids low-key instruction. Take it from me, many children don't understand that canoeing is a simple exercise in physics. They believe that paddle strokes are really a religious ritual. If they do them right, the canoe gods make the canoe go straight.

They don't understand the relations of force, resistance and symmetry. When the boat won't go straight, they believe they haven't pleased the gods, or that it is just one more example of their personal inadequacy. If you get mad on top of this, you only add to their isolation.

7. Play with your boat. Use it as a swimming platform. Swamp it. Learn the limits of when it will tip through roughhouse games. It's fun, and you will learn a lot about your boat and balance.

What to Consider Taking

This section is written for novice stream canoeists. I assume you know what to take for a camping trip, so I'll focus on stuff peculiar to boating. I'll also suggest some ways to hold down your costs of acquiring new equipment.

In any season it is important that your gear that needs to stay dry does so. It's also important that you not lose any important gear in the event of an upset. (I know. You don't plan to upset. Almost no one does. The key is to plan for it, even if you don't plan to do it.)

Ammo Cans

Traditionally used by the Armed Forces to store ammunition, these small metal cans can be bought at surplus and camping stores pretty cheap. They are waterproof. They close securely. They can be easily tied into boats. For more money it is possible to buy plastic versions that are lighter in weight.

These cans are good for your personal toiletries, cameras, short-barreled handguns, or anything you might want quick access to, or items you don't want mixed in with other gear, such as your tools or medical supplies.

Rocket Boxes

Again, these are Armed Forces surplus items. The Armed Forces uses them to store larger-sized ammo and projectiles. They are waterproof and close securely. They are great for your food boxes, camp lantern, books and other such gear. Most of these are rectangular in shape.

It is possible, though somewhat difficult, to find square ones. Square ones are good for dutch ovens and other kitchen gear that don't fit so well in the narrow rocket boxes. Rocket boxes can also be used to create portable, comfortable and very secure camp toilets.

Milk Crates

Not my personal favorite, but I have friends who pack these sturdy, open containers with canned food and other stuff that it doesn't hurt to get wet. They then weave rope over the top to hold the stuff into the crate and then tie the crate into the boat.

Waterproof Bags (also called wet bags or dry bags)

Heavy duty bags of various sizes, sold at stores that cater to boaters and through various catalogs. In these you store your sleeping bag, clothing and other stuff you really don't want to get wet. These bags are made of rubber or plastic, so they are soft sided. The gear you want dry and protected from being crushed should go into the ammo cans and rocket boxes.

Plastic Bags (inside other bags or backpacks)

Here is how the casual or new boater can imitate the benefits of waterproof bags without running out and buying them. Place the stuff you want kept dry inside a plastic bag. Press or suck all possible air out of the bag (this helps lessen the chance of tears or punctures). Seal that bag and place it inside another plastic bag, remove the air, and seal. Put the plastic bags inside a burlap bag, canvas bag or backpack to protect the plastic from general abuse and tie the whole shebang into your boat.

Strong Ropes and Straps

Take extras. It is better to carry extra ropes and straps needlessly than it is to be in a remote situation and want them. In addition to tying the boats to trees, or tying things into the boats, ropes/straps can be used to help pull boats off some midstream pin.

Life Jackets (of adequate size, design and condition)

You would think this would be obvious. Avoid "horse collar"

personal flotation devices. It is easy to slip out of them and they are not comfortable. Small children should be in life jackets which have straps that run between their legs. If you need to pull your child out of the water, and your only available grip is on their jacket, you want the kid to exit the water with the jacket. It is not uncommon for children to slip right out the bottom of a jacket in this sort of situation.

Spare paddles

One spare per boat. Don't tie it in. You may lose your grip on one of your regular paddles at an inopportune time and need to quickly grab your spare.

Saw

Some large-toothed saw that can be packed into a small space. Such saws are available in backpacking stores or hunting/fishing stores. This is for more than the possible cutting of firewood. In my experience, the most common of pins in the stream involve trees or downed wood of some sort. Often, the only way I have been able to retrieve someone's canoe has been to cut away a stump or tree limb.

Various Personal Gear

- **Strap** or tie-on for your eyeglasses.
- **Shoes** that tie securely to your feet. Take an extra pair to change into when you are done wading and to serve as a spare.
- **Extra trash bags.** You can use these to replace torn ones that were being used to keep gear dry, or to carry out trash left behind by other folk.
- **Water purification** materials.
- **Fire lids** or small stoves. Using fire lids helps keep alive the fragile grasses that hold the beaches together.
- **Duct tape** (furnace tape). It can be used to fix virtually anything. I've seen it used to patch holes in boats the size of someone's head. Don't leave home without it!
- **Hand lotion.** Lots of hand lotion. From your hands' perspective, boating is sort of like washing dishes for hours each day, for days on end. Many western streams carry skin drying chemicals and/or possess a ph balance which is hard on skin. Take lip moisturizer, also.
- **Sun tan lotion.** Arizona boating includes lots of sun, reflecting off water and your boat.

- **Hats.** Take extra. The river gods seem to demand hats as periodic sacrifice. Take ones you can soak in water and wear to help keep you cool, if the water is hot.

Cold Weather/Cold Water

I'm assuming you don't have a wet suit or a dry suit. Even if you do, you should take some of this gear. Hypothermia is a real threat. Any time the air temperature plus the water temperature totals to less than 100 degrees you should be especially wary of this killer. Even if the total temperature exceeds 100, keep an eye out for symptoms. Especially watch children, small or thin folk, or those poorly prepared for boating conditions.

- **Flares.** A highway flare, available at automotive stores, stores easily and will light virtually any available wood.
- **Extra** change of **clothes.**
- Wear clothes made of **wool**, polypropylene or some other material which will help your body retain warmth even if the clothing is wet. Cotton does just the opposite. Wet cotton is worse than no clothing at all in most situations.
- **Wool cap** and a **wool scarf.** Your most significant heat loss occurs where there is lots of blood near your skin, such as your head, neck, armpits and groin.
- **Gloves** made of wool or polypro. It helps to wear a larger glove of some material which will cut the wind over a wool or polypro glove. Another option is to carry lots of nonsterile plastic medical gloves which you wear under your wool or polypro gloves.
- **Ski pants** or the plastic sauna pants that are sometimes available (at low cost) in health food stores. These help cut the wind and keep you dry from incidental splashes.
- Small plastic **boots** or plastic to wrap your feet in before you put your feet into your shoes.

Dealing with Pinned Boats

This is a casual discussion of an important topic within the paddling community. Not only have long and detailed articles been written about it, but multi-day training courses complete with graduation certificates are out there.

Remember this. Your boat can only be badly pinned if you put you and your boat in a situation where a pin is probable. It is possible to regularly boat the Verde and substantially avoid this possibility.

Rescuing Trapped People

Do it real fast. Better yet, make sure every person on the trip knows what evasive actions to take which can virtually eliminate the chance of a person being trapped. On occasion, people are trapped simply walking across a stream. If the water is fast and somewhat high, it is possible for a foot to become tightly wedged in rocks. If a person loses balance, it has happened that the force of the river has twisted their body downstream, breaking their leg and pinning them underwater.

Obviously, getting in this unhappy situation suggests first that the person has attempted to walk across a high, fast stream. "High," incidentally need not be much over a person's knee, especially if the water is fast and the stream bed very rocky. "High" to your child may be very low indeed.

The person's upper body must be supported up out of the water. The more body out of water, the less pull the force of the current has on the person. You don't have enough strength to do this just by lifting.

If you followed my excellent suggestion to bring lots of rope and/or straps, you can usually secure each end to trees or rocks on the banks. This rope can then be made taut, located so it intersects the trapped person and is itself sufficiently above the water level to be able to provide secure support.

Sometimes the person is trapped in conjunction with the boat. Maybe the person ended up swimming downstream of an uncontrolled and/or swamped boat with both paddler and boat being swept on to a tree or rock. It's kind of like a sandwich. The person is the filling. The boat and the obstruction are the pieces of bread.

Another possibility, especially with kayaks, is that the boat, with person inside, was swept onto a rock or tree. The force of the water then collapses the boat onto the paddler's legs, and wraps boat and legs around the obstruction.

Another possibility is that the boater attempted to run a very steep, near vertical, drop and pinned the bow on a rock. Rather than the boat spinning sideways, for some reason the boat may stay in a linear position. The water rushes over the boat and pins the person, face down, underwater, to the front of the boat.

The possibility of a swimmer being trapped by being caught between a swamped boat and an obstruction is the only one which is likely at low flows. The other two possibilities usually occur at higher flows and to the boaters who dance with the river in those more challenging of times. The risk of any of these accidents occurring can be substantially reduced by not being careless and by making the right decision.

I always carry a saw on canoe or kayak trips. Using the saw I can free boat or paddler trapped against wood by sawing away the wood. I have helped retrieve boats that otherwise would have to have been left, except that we had a saw and could simply remove the obstruction. Saws can also be used, if necessary, to saw through the boats themselves, if the boat is not metal.

As mentioned earlier, you must rig a way to help the person keep his head above water. This usually means stringing ropes. Once you know the person is not immediately facing death, you can work the rest out.

Retrieving Pinned Boats

Rafts can be punctured with a knife, deflated and repaired on shore after the rescue.

Canoes and kayaks usually need to be lifted in some way. Try to get the current to work with you, not against you. Lift one end of the trapped boat up out of the water. Often the current will grab the other end and spin the boat off the obstruction. With canoes, you may have to try to spin the boat a bit to keep as much of the current as possible out of the inside of the canoe.

While rescuing people or craft, don't get downstream of the pin unless the situation is absolutely secure. A second pin involving you will not help the situation. Try to secure or remove all entangling lines, especially those with fish hooks on the end. Try to approach the situation from the sides. Don't get directly above the situation if you might get swept into it and become part of a problem.

It wouldn't hurt to do some reading on swift water rescue if you plan to boat. But, remember, you can decide what situations you will chance. If you boat low water, you can never eliminate the risk of a trapped boat. You can almost virtually remove the risk of a trapped person.

The International Whitewater Rating Scale

This scale has been standardized around the world. At least, these concepts have been standardized around the world. The application of these words has not.

Class 1

Moving water with few riffles or obstructions. Standing waves are not greater than one foot high, peak to trough.

Class 2

Small rapids with waves not greater than three feet, peak to trough. Channels are obvious and clear of obstructions. Scouting is not typically required. Maneuvering does not require the paddler to significantly fight the current.

Class 3

Powerful rapids with waves typically less than five feet, peak to trough. Scouting is advisable. Maneuvering is required, often in conflict with the push of the current, in order to miss obstacles.

Class 4

Long and difficult rapids which require intricate and precise maneuvering in turbulent, pushy water. Scouting is typically necessary. Rescue is difficult.

Class 5

Extremely difficult and violent rapids. Necessary maneuvering is difficult and requires precise boat control in violent, pushy current. Obstacles are frequent and difficult to miss. Rescue is difficult, perhaps impossible.

Class 6

The most extreme imaginable. (Some waterfalls 25 feet or greater in height are only considered Class 5.) Teams of experts run at significant risk to life.

Stream Sections Ranked by Boating Difficulty

This ranking assumes the cfs is not at flood flows. As the gauge at Camp Verde nears 300 cfs and the gauge at Tangle Creek ("Going into Horseshoe") nears 500, all of these sections are more difficult.

If a wave of water is traveling down the watershed, it is possible that one of the tributaries could be dangerously high while the gauge at Camp Verde is still at a safe level. When in doubt, stay safe.

This ranking is for the stream segment as a whole. Individual rapids or situations within the segment could be more difficult than the ranking indicates.

Finally, this ranking does not factor in the effects of weather or isolated location. If a section is listed as "shallow," boaters should anticipate getting out of their craft to drag through shallows at the regularly-occurring flows.

Easy Sections: Class 1 through Low Class 2

Verde River

- Morgan Ranch to Perkinsville (shallow water).
- Perkinsville to TAPCO (shallow water).
- Dead Horse Park to Bridgeport (shallow water).
- Bridgeport to Oak Creek.
- Oak Creek to Camp Verde.
- Camp Verde to Beasley Flats.
- Horseshoe Dam to Bartlett Dam.
- Bartlett Dam to Salt River.

Oak Creek

- Cornville to Verde River (shallow water).

Beaver Creek

● Montezuma Castle to Verde River.

Medium Sections:
Low Class 2 to High Class 2

Verde River

● Beasley Flats to Childs (under 300 cfs at Camp Verde).
● Childs to Horseshoe Dam (under 500 cfs at Tangle Creek).

Oak Creek

● Page Springs to Cornville.

Beaver Creek

● Confluence of Wet/Dry to Montezuma Castle.

High Class 2 and 3

Hard Sections or Contains Strainers

Verde River

● Beasley Flats to Childs (above 300 cfs at Camp Verde).
● Childs to Horseshoe Dam (above 500 cfs at Tangle Creek).

Oak Creek

● All sections above Page Springs.

Wet Beaver Creek

● All sections.

   I did not forget a section. If I did not list it, I am recommending you not even consider paddling it until you know for a fact that you are a strong, competent whitewater paddler.

Glossary
Explanations and Self-Righteous Assertions

AGFD: Arizona Game and Fish Department.

Bait Bucket Charlie: A slang term for individuals who, without authorization from AGFD, add live fish to some body of water.

CFS: Cubic Feet per Second. If you stand at a point on the river and watch the water, "cfs" refers to the amount of water you watch roll by.

Closed or Decked Canoes: A double-pointed craft propelled by a single blade paddle. Paddlers wear a waterproof skirt which attaches to the deck of the boat. The paddler is locked into a kneeling position, subject to purification by pain. I believe these paddlers are folk who committed the sins of being kayakers or inflatable paddlers in some past life.

Cottonwood Bench: A raised river bank, more or less flat on top, which sports a growth of cottonwoods.

Creek, Crick, River: By some standards, the Verde is never a full grown river. I use these terms as synonyms throughout the book.

FR followed by a number (for example, FR 32): This means Forest Road with a specific identification number. These are recognized roads of the U.S. Forest Service. Being recognized does not mean that they are maintained or passable.

FRM followed by a number (for example, FRM 22): Forest River Mile 22. On the map the Forest Serice provides to river runners on the Verde. They start counting at Horseshoe Dam and add as they travel upstream to Camp Verde. AGFD starts numbering at the same point and the same way but continues up past Morgan Ranch.

Gauge Names: If you see something like this: 555 cfs (Camp Verde): I mean 555 cfs at the Camp Verde USGS gauge. The gauges typically mentioned are Camp Verde, Tangle Creek, going into Horseshoe Lake, below Horseshoe Dam, and below Bartlett Dam. In the preceding sentences, I have attempted to use the words you are likely to hear when you call the SRP information line. They do sometimes vary the words, but these are typical.

Head Winds: An upstream wind which separates wheat paddlers from chaff paddlers and reminds all of us of our humanity. Paddlers who encounter days of headwinds should consider prayers of repentance and perhaps the sacrificial offering of a kayaker or inflatable paddler.

Holes: A hydrologic phenomena created when water rushing over some obstruction punches a hole in the water downstream of the obstruction. Water immediately surrounding this point of impact will flow into the area in an attempt to fill in the void.

Raft Potato: River runners incapable of learning how to paddle an inflatable. Amazingly, not all of these folk are infants.

Inflatables: Double-pointed rafts designed for one or two paddlers. Propelled from a seated position, using a double blade paddle. This craft is designed for those who find kayaks difficult to master.

Kayaks: A double-pointed, decked-over boat propelled by a double-blade paddle. The paddler is fixed into a seated position. This is a good craft for those who can't figure which end of the paddle to put in the water. Appropriately locked into a seated position, kayakers paddle beneath the gaze of all canoeists. This is also the craft for slow learners, as kayakers need learn only about half the strokes required of canoeists.

Lateral Waves: Waves which come at a diagonal off the banks of the river.

Minimum Stream Flow: The minimum amount of water that can possibly be left flowing down a stream bed that will still maintain a living riparian zone.

Open Canoes: This is the craft that Americans identify as a canoe. Narrow, pointed at both ends, open to the heavens, it is propelled by a single-blade paddle or pole. Canoes are the most beautiful and advanced of all water craft. They allow the paddler to sit, stand or kneel. They have a good bit of cargo space and can be used in shallow, narrow streams. Canoes can be used by young, old and partially-handicapped. They allow maneuverability while demanding skill.

Pillow: When flowing water encounters a stationary, solid object, such as a rock, the water piles up on the upstream side before flowing around the object. That pile of water is called a "pillow."

Rafts: Large barges, useful on large rivers for carrying gear and raft potatoes. Never insult a rafter, unless you want to carry all your own gear.

Rapid Names: All of the names can be divided into three categories: 1) Those used by the local paddling community; 2) Those used by the Forest Service on their maps; and 3) The ones I am trying to promote on the world. I'll try to keep the categories straight for you.

River Right, River Left: On the river **ALL** directions are ALWAYS given as if you were looking **downstream**, even if you are looking upstream. In this book, all references to right or left refer to a river right and a river left, even if I delete the word "river."

Strainers/Sweepers: Any obstruction, most often trees, which allow the water to pass through while trapping solid objects, such as boats and boaters.

SRP: Salt River Project. Utility company that supplies water to the Phoenix metro area.

TRM followed by a number (for example, TRM 8): This means Total River Mile 8. This refers to the total (approximate) miles the Verde has flowed from the highest point that it is perennial, which also happens to be the highest point at which it is possible.

I'm not sure exactly how long the Verde is. It's a confusion I share with many. AGFD biologists have told me about 185 miles. I measured it out to about 195. A friend of mine measured it out to 191. Other figures I've read speak of 160 or 174.

Much of the variance seems to depend on the assumptions made when measuring the distance through the lakes. Do you chart the straightest possible path? Or, do you follow the course of the original river bed. I followed the course of that drowned river bed.

USGS: United States Geological Survey.

Wilderness/wilderness. Wild/wild. Scenic/scenic: Whenever these words are capitalized in an otherwise inappropriate spot, I am referring to a legal, Federal government designation. In other words, Wilderness is land designed as such by the Federal Government and managed in such a way to maintain a wilderness character. When I talked about wilderness, I'm referring to some extraordinarily remote area, which has not been added to the Fed's Wilderness system. Wild and Scenic are designations in the Federal Wild and Scenic River System. There are three designators in that system: Recreational, Scenic and Wild. Wild refers to the character of the land near the river, not to the presence of rapids.

Map Reference

Boaters, sportsmen and other recreationists who want more detailed information on the Verde should obtain the following maps:

Morgan Ranch to Perkinsville
U.S. Forest: Prescott
USGS topos (7.5): Chino Valley North, Paulden, Perkinsville, King Canyon

Perkinsville to TAPCO
U.S. Forest: Prescott, Coconino
USGS topos (7.5): Perkinsville, Clarkdale

TAPCO to Dead Horse Park
U.S. Forest: Prescott, Coconino
U.S. topos (7.5): Clarkdale, Cottonwood

Dead Horse to Bridgeport
U.S. Forest: Coconino, Prescott
USGS topos (7.5): Clarkdale, Cottonwood, Cornville

Bridgeport to Oak Creek
U.S. Forest: Prescott, Coconino
USGS topo (7.5): Cornville

Oak Creek to Camp Verde
U.S. Forest: Prescott, Coconino
USGS topo (7.5): Clarkdale, Cottonwood, Cornville, Middle Verde

Camp Verde to Beasley Flats
U.S. Forest: Prescott, Coconino
Recreation Opportunity Guide: Verde River (available from the Verde District Ranger Station in Camp Verde)
USGS topo (7.5): Cornville, Middle Verde, Camp Verde, Horner Mountain

Beasley Flats to Childs
U.S. Forest: Prescott, Coconino
Recreation Opportunity Guide: Verde River
USGS topo (7.5): Horner Mountain, Hackberry Mountain, Verde Hot Springs

Childs to Horseshoe Dam
U.S. Forest: Prescott, Coconino, Tonto
Recreation Opportunity Guide: Verde River
USGS topo (7.5): Verde Hot Springs, Wet Bottom,
  Chalk Mountain, Horseshoe Dam

Horseshoe Dam to Bartlett Dam
U.S. Forest: Tonto
USGS topo (7.5): Horseshoe Dam, Lion Mountain,
  Maverick Mountain, Bartlett Dam

Bartlett Dam to Salt River
U.S. Forest: Tonto
USGS topo (7.5): Bartlett Dam, Fort McDowell,
Granite Reef

These maps cover the Verde River. If you wish to explore the tributaries, you may need to buy additional, different maps.

Mother and daughter team.

Rentals and Outfitters

There exists a rental outlet, outfitter or guide for every possible (legal) desire. Whether your interest is birds, fish, hunting, archaeological sites, four-wheeling, hiking, mountain bikes, boating, following old movie trails, or painting, there is at least one business or nonprofit organization in Arizona that is eager to help you explore the lands and waters of the Verde Watershed.

Businesses come and go. For up-to-date lists of businesses and nonprofit organizations that hold permits to do business on U.S. Forest land, contact the district office of the particular Forest you are interested in. (In some cases the list is 10 pages long.) Then contact the ones that seem to have what you want.

Listed below are companies that rent boating equipment and/or offer guiding/outfitting services for some sections of the Verde River. The notes to the right are based on the **past** practice of the firm and are subject to change.

WatersEdge Inflatables
P.O. Box 77692
Tucson, AZ 85703
1-800-999-RAFT 1-602-744-8818

Rents catarafts, other rafts, inflatables, sea kayaks, and a wide variety of other gear. Offers complete expedition outfitting to the Grand Canyon and other southwestern rivers.

Cimarron Adventures
David Insley
7714 East Catalina Drive
Scottsdale, AZ 85251
(602) 994-1199 (602) 352-4460

Outfits and guides trips.
Operates year-round
below Bartlett Dam.

Desert Voyagers
Pat Blumm
P.O. Box 9053
Scottsdale, AZ 85252
(602) 998-7238
1-800-222-RAFT

Outfits and guides trips,
mostly rafts & inflatables.
Mostly at high water. Covers
from Verde Valley down to Salt
River. Year-round below the dams.

Down River Canoe Rental
Larry Landry
HC 62, Box 179
Camp Verde, AZ 86322
(602) 567-6531

Whenever CFS is above 65,
rents Dagger canoes, canoeing
gear, and shuttle services.
Operates in Verde Valley area.

River Otter Canoe Rental
Rich Shafer
P.O. Box 2656
Camp Verde, AZ 86322
(602) 567-4116

Rents Coleman canoes and
provides shuttle services.
Provides river access and
camping to all interested
river runners.

Continued on next page . . .

Continued from previous page:

Verde River Canyon Excursion Train
300 N. Broadway
P.O. Box 103
Clarkdale, AZ 86324
(602) 639-0010
1-800-858-RAIL (7245)

Offers scenic train trips at slow speeds between Clarkdale and Perkinsville. A comfortable and entertaining way to see one of the most beautiful sections of the Verde.

Information Sources
Canoeing Instruction Resources

Mason, Bill. *Path of the Paddle*. Toronto: Key Porter Books
Stone, Ken. *Guide to Canoeing*. L. L. Beane Video

U.S. Forest Service District Offices

Tonto National Forest
Cave Creek District Office
P.O. Box 768
Carefree, AZ 85331
(602) 488-3441

Coconino National Forest
Beaver Creek District
HC 64, Box 240
Rimrock, AZ 86335
(602) 567-4501

Prescott National Forest
Chino Valley Dist. Office
P.O. Box 485
Chino Valley, AZ 86323
(602) 636-2302

Prescott National Forest
Verde District Office
P.O. Box 670
Camp Verde, AZ 86322
(602) 567-4121

At present, private trips do not need a permit to run any section of the Verde. Trips are limited to 15 people in a single group in the Wild and Scenic stretch. This may change. Call the U.S. Forest Service District Office covering your section of the river for current information.

Other Sources

Arizona Game & Fish Department
2222 West Greenway
Phoenix, AZ 85023
(602) 942-3000

Camp Verde Chamber of Commerce
P.O. Box 1665
Camp Verde, AZ 86322
(602) 567-9294

SRP Lakes and Rivers Report
(602) 236-5929 (recorded)

State Land Commissioner
1616 West Adams
Phoenix, AZ 85007

Verde Valley Chamber of Commerce
1010 South Main Street
Cottonwood, AZ 86326
(602) 282-6722

Selected Bibliography

Arizona Public Service Co., Phoenix. Historial Files.

Arizona State Parks. *Arizona Rivers and Streams Guide.* Phoenix: Arizona State Parks, 1989.

Benson, Lyman. *The Cacti of Arizona.* Tucson: The University of Arizona Press, 1981.

Benson, Lyman and Robert A. Darrow. *Trees and Shrubs of the Southwest Deserts.* Tucson: The University of Arizona Press, 1981.

Brown, David E. *Arizona Game Birds.* Tucson: The University of Arizona Press, 1989.

Brown, David E. *Arizona Wetlands & Waterfowl.* Tucson: The University of Arizona Press, 1985.

Davis, Barbara L. *Birds of the Southwest* (Vol. 1). Tucson: Treasure Chest Publications, Inc., 1986.

Day, Gerald. *Javelina Research & Management in Arizona.* Phoenix: Arizona Game & Fish Department, 1985.

Desert Botanical Garden Staff. *Desert Wildflowers.* Phoenix: Arizona Highways, 1988.

Duffield, Mary Rose and Warren P. Jones. *Plants for Dry Climates.* Tucson: H.P. Books, 1981.

Harris, Rick. *Explore Arizona!* Phoenix: Golden West Publishers, 1990.

Heatwole, Thelma. *Arizona Hideaways.* Phoenix: Golden West Publishers, 1986.

Heymann, M. M. *Reptiles and Amphibians of the American Southwest.* Pico Rivera: Gem Guides Book Co., 1975.

River gods demand periodic sacrifice.

Hoffmeister, Donald. *Mammals of Arizona.* Phoenix: Arizona Game & Fish Department and Tucson: The University of Arizona Press, 1986.

Levi, Herbert and Lorna Levi. *A Golden Guide: Spiders and their Kin.* New York: Golden Press, 1987.

Lowe, Charles H. and others. *The Venomous Reptiles of Arizona.* Phoenix: Arizona Game and Fish Department, 1986.

Minckley, W. L. *Fishes of Arizona.* Phoenix: Arizona Game & Fish Department, 1973.

Parker Kittie. *Illustrated Guide of Arizona Weeds.* Tucson: The University of Arizona Press, 1972.

Recreation Opportunity Guide: Verde River. U.S. Dept. of Agriculture (Coconino, Prescott & Tonto National Forests), 1990.

Robbins, Chandler and others. *Birds of North America.* New York: Golden Press, 1966.

Shaw, Harley and others. *Factors Affecting Mountain Lion Densities and Cattle Depredation in Arizona.* Phoenix: Arizona Game & Fish Department, 1988.

Shaw, Harley. *Mountain Lion Field Guide* (Special Report #9). Phoenix: Arizona Game & Fish Department, 1983.

Snyder, Ernest E. *Arizona Outdoor Guide.* Phoenix: Golden West Publishers, 1985.

Snyder, Ernest E. *Prehistoric Arizona.* Phoenix: Golden West Publishers, 1987.

"Verde River Day Supplemental, 1989." *The Verde Independent,* September 27, 1989.

Woolsey, Norma G. *Coyote Field Guide* (Special Report #15). Phoenix: Arizona Game & Fish Department, 1985.

Dad wins a game of canoe tag.

INDEX

U - V

W - Z

Meet the Author!

Jim Slingluff is the first person to make a continuous canoe descent of the entire Verde River. He has also canoed sections of the Salt River, Dry Beaver, Wet Beaver and Oak Creeks.

Jim learned to canoe as a Boy Scout at the age of thirteen. Over the years he has kayaked and canoed many whitewater rivers country, including the Potomac, Shenandoah and Cheat Rivers, and the Colorado through the Grand Canyon, as well as many smaller streams.

Slingluff was a member of Team Grand Canyon which took a silver medal in international competition in downriver/orienteering on rivers in North Carolina, Tennessee and Georgia in 1990.

He is a member of Sonoran Arthropod Studies, National Rifle Association, Arizona Riparian Council, Arizona and National Wildlife Federations, Tucson Rod and Gun Club, Northern Arizona Paddlers Club, Central Arizona Paddlers Club and Nature Conservancy.

He has done volunteer work for the U.S. Forest Service, Native Fish Program of the Arizona Game and Fish Department, and the Statewide Comprehensive Outdoor Recreation Plan.

Jim Slingluff has been appointed by Governor Symington to represent recreationists on the Riparian Areas Advisory Council. This Council is charged by law with developing suggested legislation to protect the riparian zones of Arizona.

He also intends to be involved in making sure the Navigable Stream Adjudication Commission is fully aware of the public values associated with riparian recreation.

Readers who wish to give Jim suggestions on riparian issues, or this book, should contact Jim through Golden West Publishers.

Jim and his wife, Beth, reside in Tucson where he is affiliated with the Arizona Education Association. He has combined his hobbies of birdwatching, canoeing, hunting, fishing, hiking and starwatching with his skills and experiences to write his first book—*Verde River Recreation Guide*.

More Great Books from Golden West Publishers!

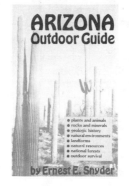

ARIZONA OUTDOOR GUIDE

Guide to plants, animals, birds, rocks, minerals, geologic history, natural environments, landforms, resources, national forests and outdoor survival. Maps, photos, drawings, charts, index. *Arizona Outdoor Guide* by Ernest E. Snyder. (128 pages) . . . **$5.95**

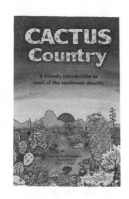

CACTUS COUNTRY

Before you touch, read this fascinating book on cactus of the southwest deserts. The many illustrations and humorous cartoons make this trip through the desert one to remember! *Cactus Country* by Jim and Sue Willoughby (112 pages) . . . **$6.95**

SNAKES and other REPTILES

This book is a must for hikers, hunters, campers and all outdoor enthusiasts! More than 80 photographs and illustrations in the text and full color plate insert, this book is the definitive, easy-to-use guide to Southwestern reptiles! *Snakes and other Reptiles* by Erik Stoops and Annette Wright (128 pages) . . . **$9.95**

FISHING ARIZONA

Noted outdoors writer G. J. Sagi takes you fishing on 50 of Arizona's most popular lakes and streams revealing when, where and how to catch those lunkers! Current catch records. *Fishing Arizona* by G. J. Sagi (160 pages) . . . **$7.95**

ORDER BLANK
Golden West Publishers

☼ 4113 N. Longview Ave. — Phoenix, AZ 85014

602-265-4392 • **1-800-658-5830** • FAX 602-279-6901

Qty.	TITLE	Per Copy	AMOUNT
	Arizona Adventure	5.95	
	Arizona Cook Book	5.95	
	Arizona Crosswords	4.95	
	Arizona Museums	9.95	
	Arizona—Off the Beaten Path	5.95	
	Arizona Outdoor Guide	5.95	
	Cactus Country	6.95	
	Discover Arizona	6.95	
	Explore Arizona	6.95	
	Fishing Arizona	7.95	
	Ghost Towns in Arizona	5.95	
	Hiking Arizona	6.95	
	Prehistoric Arizona	5.00	
	Quest for the Dutchman's Gold	6.95	
	Snakes and Other Reptiles of the SW	9.95	
	Verde River Recreation Guide	6.95	
	Wild West Characters	6.95	
Add $2.00 to total order for shipping & handling			**$2.00**

☐ My Check or Money Order Enclosed. . . . . $ _____

☐ MasterCard   ☐ VISA

Acct. No. _____ Exp. Date _____

Signature _____

Name _____ Phone _____

Address _____

City/State/Zip _____

MasterCard and VISA Orders Accepted ($20 Minimum)

Call for Free Golden West Catalog

2/93

VerdeRiver

This order blank may be photo-copied.